THE MASK

"A master of sheer fright!" — *Florida Times-Union*

Don't miss these other hair-raising thrillers by Dean R. Koontz . . .

WATCHERS

"Thoroughly frightening and entertaining . . . His best story yet!" — *Publishers Weekly*

"The suspense holds to the end!" — *New York Times*

"A breakthrough for Koontz . . . imaginative and unusual." — *Kirkus*

"Unrelentingly suspenseful . . . first class entertainment!" — *Cleveland Plain Dealer*

TWILIGHT EYES

"A spine-chilling adventure . . . will keep you turning pages to the very end." — *Rave Reviews*

"Chilling . . . superbly scary." — *Los Angeles Times*

"Terrific scares and action!" — *Fangoria*

Continued . . .

NIGHT CHILLS

"As fast and exciting as any thriller you have ever read."
— *King Features Syndicate*

"As frightening as *PSYCHO.*" — *Minneapolis Tribune*

"Will send chills down your back." — *New York Times*

DARKFALL

"A fast-paced tale . . . one of the scariest chase scenes ever!" — *Houston Post*

"Swift, entertaining . . . a classic race to the rescue."
— *Publishers Weekly*

THE VISION

"Spine-tingling—it gives you an almost lethal shock."
— *San Francisco Chronicle*

"Hair-raising . . . The tension never lets up!"
— *Florida Times-Union*

THE FACE OF FEAR

"A real nail-biter!" — *Library Journal*

"Real suspense . . . tension upon tension."
— *New York Times*

THE MASK

DEAN R. KOONTZ

BERKLEY BOOKS, NEW YORK

The Mask was previously published under
the pseudonym of Owen West.

THE MASK

A Berkley Book / published by arrangement with
Nkui, Inc. c/o Harold Ober Associates

PRINTING HISTORY
Jove edition / November 1981
Berkley edition / December 1988

ISBN: 0-425-09777-3

A BERKLEY BOOK ® TM 757,375
Berkley Books are published by The Berkley Publishing Group,
200 Madison Avenue, New York, New York 10016.
The name "BERKLEY" and the "B" logo
are trademarks belonging to Berkley Publishing Corporation.

PRINTED IN THE UNITED STATES OF AMERICA

10 9 8 7 6 5 4 3 2

This book is dedicated to
Willo and Dave Roberts
and to
Carol and Don McQuinn
who have no faults—
except that they live
too far away from us

A dirge for her, the doubly dead, in that
    she died so young.
                —Edgar Allan Poe, "Lenore"

And much of Madness, and more of Sin,
And Horror the soul of the plot.
                —Edgar Allan Poe, "The Conqueror Worm"

Extreme terror gives us back the
gestures of our childhood.
                —Chazal

THE MASK

Prologue

LAURA was in the cellar, doing some spring cleaning and hating every minute of it. She didn't dislike the work itself; she was by nature an industrious girl who was happiest when she had chores to do. But she was afraid of the cellar.

For one thing, the place was gloomy. The four narrow windows, set high in the walls, were hardly larger than embrasures, and the dust-filmed panes of glass permitted only weak, chalky light to enter. Even brightened by a pair of lamps, the big room held on tenaciously to its shadows, unwilling to be completely disrobed. The flickering amber light from the lamps revealed damp stone walls and a hulking, coal-fired furnace that was cold and unused on this fine, warm May afternoon. On a series of long shelves, row upon row of quart jars reflected splinters of light, but their contents—home-canned fruit and vegetables that had been stored here for the past nine months—remained unilluminated. The corners of the room were all dark, and the low, open-beamed ceiling was hung with shadows like long banners of funeral crepe.

The cellar always had a mildly unpleasant odor, too. It was musty, rather like a limestone cave. In the spring and summer, when the humidity was high, a mottled gray-green fungus sometimes sprang up in the corners, a disgusting scablike growth, fringed with hundreds of tiny white spores that resembled insect eggs; that grotesquery added its own thin but nonetheless displeasing fragrance to the cellar air.

However, neither the gloom nor the offending odors nor the fungus gave rise to Laura's fears; it was the spiders that frightened her. Spiders ruled the cellar. Some of them were small, brown, and quick; others were charcoal gray, a bit bigger than the brown ones, but just as fast-moving as their smaller cousins. There were even a few blue-black giants as large as Laura's thumb.

As she wiped dust and a few cobwebs from the jars of home-canned food, always alert for the scuttling movement of spiders, Laura grew increasingly angry with her mother. Mama could have let her clean some of the upstairs rooms instead of the cellar; Aunt Rachael or Mama herself could have cleaned down here because neither of them worried about spiders. But Mama knew that Laura was afraid of the cellar, and Mama was in the mood to punish her. It was a terrible mood, black as thunderclouds. Laura had seen it before. Too often. It descended over Mama more frequently with every passing year, and when she was in its thrall, she was a different person from the smiling, always singing woman that she was at other times. Although Laura loved her mother, she did not love the short-tempered, mean-spirited woman that her mother sometimes became. She did not love the hateful woman who had sent her down into the cellar with the spiders.

Dusting the jars of peaches, pears, tomatoes, beets, beans, and pickled squash, nervously awaiting the inevitable appearance of a spider, wishing she were grown up and married and on her own, Laura was startled by a sudden, sharp sound that pierced the dank basement air. At first it was like the distant, forlorn wail of an exotic bird, but it quickly became louder and more urgent. She stopped dusting, looked up at the dark ceiling, and listened closely to the eerie ululation that came from overhead. After a moment she realized that it was her Aunt Rachael's voice and that it was a cry of alarm.

Upstairs, something fell over with a crash. It sounded like shattering porcelain. It must have been Mama's peacock vase. If it was the vase, Mama would be in an *extremely* foul mood for the rest of the week.

Laura stepped away from the shelves of canned goods and started toward the cellar stairs, but she stopped abruptly when she heard Mama scream. It wasn't a scream of rage over the loss of the vase; there was a note of terror in it.

Footsteps thumped across the living room floor, toward the front door of the house. The screen door opened with the familiar singing of its long spring, then banged shut. Rachael was outside now, shouting, her words unintelligible but still conveying her fear.

Laura smelled smoke.

She hurried to the stairs and saw pale tongues of

fire at the top. The smoke wasn't heavy, but it had an acrid stench.

Heart pounding, Laura climbed to the uppermost step. Waves of heat forced her to squint, but she could see into the kitchen. The wall of fire wasn't solid. There was a narrow route of escape, a corridor of cool safety; the door to the back porch was at the far end.

She lifted her long skirt and pulled it tight across her hips and thighs, bunching it in both hands to prevent it from trailing in the flames. She moved gingerly onto the fire-ringed landing, which creaked under her, but before she reached the open door, the kitchen exploded in yellow-blue flames that quickly turned orange. From wall to wall, floor to ceiling, the room was an inferno; there was no longer a path through the blaze. Crazily, the fire-choked doorway brought to Laura's mind the image of a glittering eye in a jack-o'-lantern.

In the kitchen, windows exploded, and the fire eddied in the sudden change of drafts, pushing through the cellar door, lashing at Laura. Startled, she stumbled backwards, off the landing. She fell. Turning, she grabbed at the railing, missed it, and stumbled down the short flight, cracking her head against the stone floor at the bottom.

She held on to consciousness as if it were a raft and she a drowning swimmer. When she was certain she wouldn't faint, she got to her feet. Pain coruscated across the top of her head. She raised one hand to her brow and found a trickle of blood, a small abrasion. She was dizzy and confused.

During the minute or less that she had been incapacitated, fire had spread across the entire landing at the head of the stairs. It was moving down onto the first step.

She couldn't keep her eyes focused. The rising stairs and the descending fire repeatedly blurred together in an orange haze.

Ghosts of smoke drifted down the stairwell. They reached out with long, insubstantial arms, as if to embrace Laura.

She cupped her hands around her mouth. "Help!"

No one answered.

"Somebody help me! I'm in the cellar!"

Silence.

"Aunt Rachael! Mama! For God's sake, somebody help me!"

The only response was the steadily increasing roar of the fire.

Laura had never felt so alone before. In spite of the tides of heat washing over her, she felt cold inside. She shivered.

Although her head throbbed worse than ever, and although the abrasion above her right eye continued to weep blood, at least she was having less trouble keeping her eyes focused. The problem was that she didn't like what she saw.

She stood statue-still, transfixed by the deadly spectacle of the flames. Fire crawled lizardlike down the steps, one by one, and it slithered up the rail posts, then crept down the rail with a crisp, chuckling sound.

The smoke reached the bottom of the steps and enfolded her. She coughed, and the coughing aggravated the pain in her head, making her dizzy again. She put one hand against the wall to steady herself.

Everything was happening too fast. The house was going up like a pile of well-seasoned tinder.

I'm going to die here.

That thought jolted her out of her trance. She wasn't ready to die. She was far too young. There was so much of life ahead of her, so many wonderful things to do, things she had long dreamed about doing. It wasn't fair. She *refused* to die.

She gagged on the smoke. Turning away from the burning stairs, she put a hand over her nose and mouth, but that didn't help much.

She saw flames at the far end of the cellar, and for an instant she thought she was already encircled and that all hope of rescue was gone. She cried out in despair, but then she realized the blaze hadn't found its way into the other end of the room after all. The two points of fire that she was seeing were only the twin oil lamps that had provided her with light. The flames in the lamps were harmless, safely ensconced in tall glass chimneys.

She coughed violently again, and the pain in her head settled down behind her eyes. She found it difficult to concentrate. Her thoughts were like droplets of quicksilver, sliding over one another and changing shape so often and so fast that she couldn't make sense of some of them.

She prayed silently and fervently.

Directly overhead, the ceiling groaned and appeared to *shift*. For a few seconds she held her breath, clenched her teeth, and stood with her hands fisted at her sides, waiting to be buried in rubble. But then she saw that the ceiling wasn't going to collapse— not yet.

Trembling, whimpering softly, she scurried to the nearest of the four high-set windows. It was rectangular, approximately eight inches from sill to top and eighteen inches from sash to sash, much too small to provide her with a means of escape. The other three windows were identical to the first; there was no use even taking a closer look at them.

The air was becoming less breathable by the second. Laura's sinuses ached and burned. Her mouth was filled with the revulsive, bitter taste of the smoke.

For too long she stood beneath the window, staring up in frustration and confusion at the meager, milky light that came through the dirty pane and through the haze of smoke that pressed tightly against the glass. She had the feeling she was overlooking an obvious and convenient escape hatch; in fact she was sure of it. There *was* a way out, and it had nothing to do with the windows, but she couldn't get her mind *off* the windows; she was fixated on them, just as she had been fixated on the sight of the advancing flames a couple of minutes ago. The pain in her head and behind her eyes throbbed more powerfully than ever, and with each agonizing pulsation, her thoughts became more muddled.

I'm going to die here.

A frightening vision flashed through her mind. She saw herself afire, her dark hair turned blond by the flames that consumed it and standing straight up on her head as if it were not hair but the wick of a candle. In the vision, she saw her face melting like wax, bubbling and steaming and liquefying, the features flowing together until her face no longer resembled that of a human being, until it was the hideously twisted countenance of a leering demon with empty eye sockets.

No!

She shook her head, dispelling the vision.

She was dizzy and getting dizzier. She needed a draught of clean air to rinse out her polluted lungs, but with each breath she drew more smoke than she had drawn last time. Her chest ached.

Nearby, a rhythmic pounding began; the noise was

even louder than her heartbeat, which drummed thunderously in her ears.

She turned in a circle, gagging and coughing, searching for the source of the hammering sound, striving to regain control of herself, struggling hard to *think*.

The hammering stopped.

"Laura . . ."

Above the incessant roar of the fire, she heard someone calling her name.

"Laura . . ."

"I'm down here . . . in the cellar!" she shouted. But the shout came out as nothing more than a whispered croak. Her throat was constricted and already raw from the harsh smoke and the fiercely hot air.

The effort required to stay on her feet became too great for her. She sank to her knees on the stone floor, slumped against the wall, and slid down until she was lying on her side.

"Laura . . ."

The pounding began again. A fist beating on a door.

Laura discovered that the air at floor level was cleaner than that which she had been breathing. She gasped frantically, grateful for this reprieve from suffocation.

For a few seconds the throbbing pain behind her eyes abated, and her thoughts cleared, and she remembered the outside entrance to the cellar, a pair of doors slant-set against the north wall of the house. They were locked from the inside, so that no one could get in to rescue her; in the panic and confusion she had forgotten about those doors. But now, if she kept her wits about her, she would be able to save herself.

"Laura!" It was Aunt Rachael's voice.

Laura crawled to the northwest corner of the room, where the doors sloped down at the top of a short flight of steps. She kept her head low, breathing the tainted but adequate air near the floor. The edges of the mortared stones tore her dress and scraped skin off her knees.

To her left, the entire stairwell was burning now, and flames were spreading across the wooden ceiling. Refracted and diffused by the smoky air, the firelight glowed on all sides of Laura, creating the illusion that she was crawling through a narrow tunnel of flames. At the rate the blaze was spreading, the illusion would soon be fact.

Her eyes were swollen and watery, and she wiped at them as she inched toward escape. She couldn't see very much. She used Aunt Rachael's voice as a beacon and otherwise relied on instinct.

"Laura!" The voice was near. Right above her.

She felt along the wall until she located the setback in the stone. She moved into that recess, onto the first step, lifted her head, but could see nothing: the darkness here was seamless.

"Laura, answer me. Baby, are you in there?"

Rachael was hysterical, screaming so loudly and pounding on the outside doors with such persistence that she wouldn't have heard a response even if Laura had been capable of making one.

Where was Mama? Why wasn't Mama pounding on the door, too? Didn't Mama care?

Crouching in that cramped, hot, lightless space, Laura reached up and put her hand against one of the two slant-set doors above her head. The sturdy barrier quivered and rattled under the impact of Rachael's small fists. Laura groped blindly for the latch. She put her hand over the warm metal fixture—and squarely over something else, too. Something strange and unexpected. Something that squirmed and was alive. Small but *alive.* She jerked convulsively and pulled her hand away. But the thing she touched had shifted its grip from the latch to her flesh, and it came away from the door when she withdrew her hand. It skittered out of her palm and over her thumb and across the back of her hand and along her wrist and under the sleeve of her dress before she could brush it away.

A spider.

She couldn't see it, but she knew what it was. A spider. One of the really big ones, as large as her thumb, a plump black body that glistened like a fat drop of oil, inky black and ugly. For a moment she froze, unable even to draw a breath.

She felt the spider moving up her arm, and its bold advance snapped her into action. She slapped at it through the sleeve of her dress, but she missed. The spider bit her above the crook of her arm, and she winced at the tiny nip of pain, and the disgusting creature scurried into her armpit. It bit her there, too, and suddenly she felt as though she was living through her worst nightmare, for she feared spiders more than she feared anything else on earth—certainly more than she feared fire, for in her desperate attempt to kill the spider, she had forgotten all about the burning house that was dissolving into ruin above her— and she flailed in panic, lost her balance, rolled backwards off the steps, into the main room of the cellar, cracking one hip on the stone floor. The spider tickled its way along the inside of her bodice until it was between her breasts. She screamed but could make no sound whatsoever. She put a hand to her bosom and pressed hard, and even through the fabric she could feel the spider squirming angrily against the palm of her hand, and she could feel its frenzied struggle even more directly on her bare breast, to which it was pressed, but she persisted until at last she crushed it, and she gagged again, but this time not merely because of the smoke.

For several seconds after killing the spider, she lay on the floor in a tight fetal position, shuddering violently and uncontrollably. The repulsive, wet mass of the smashed spider slid very slowly down the curve of her breast. She wanted to reach inside her bodice and pluck the foul wad from herself, but she hesitated because, irrationally, she was afraid it would somehow come to life again and sting her fingers.

She tasted blood. She had bitten her lip.

Mama...

Mama had done this to her. Mama had sent her down here, knowing there were spiders. Why was Mama always so quick to deal out punishment, so eager to assign penance?

Overhead, a beam creaked, sagged. The kitchen floor cracked open. She felt as though she were staring up into Hell. Sparks showered down. Her dress caught fire, and she scorched her hands putting it out.

Mama did this to me.

Because her palms and fingers were blistered and peeling, she couldn't crawl on her hands and knees any longer, so she got to her feet, although standing up required more strength and determination than she had thought she possessed. She swayed, dizzy and weak.

Mama sent me down here.

Laura could see only pulsing, all-encompassing orange luminescence, through which amorphous smoke ghosts glided and whirled. She shuffled toward the short flight of steps that led to the outside cellar doors, but after she had gone only two yards, she realized she was headed in the wrong direction. She turned back the way she had come—or back the way she *thought* she had come—but after a few steps she bumped into the furnace, which was nowhere near the outside doors. She was completely disoriented.

Mama did this to me.

Laura squeezed her ruined hands into raw, bloody fists. In a rage she pounded on the furnace, and with each blow she fervently wished that she were beating her mother.

The upper reaches of the burning house twisted and rumbled. In the distance, beyond an eternity of smoke, Aunt Rachael's voice echoed hauntingly: "Laura . . . Laura . . ."

Why wasn't Mama out there helping Rachael break down the cellar doors? Where in God's name *was* she? Throwing coal and lamp oil on the fire?

Wheezing, gasping, Laura pushed away from the furnace and tried to follow Rachael's voice to safety.

A beam tore loose of its moorings, slammed into her back, and catapulted her into the shelves of home-canned food. Jars fell, shattered. Laura went down in a rain of glass. She could smell pickles, peaches.

Before she could determine if any bones were broken, before she could even lift her face out of the spilled food, another beam crashed down, pinning her legs.

There was so much pain that her mind simply

blanked it out altogether. She was not even sixteen years old, and there was only so much she could bear. She sealed the pain in a dark corner of her mind; instead of succumbing to it, she twisted and thrashed hysterically, raged at her fate, and cursed her mother.

Her hatred for her mother wasn't rational, but it was so passionately felt that it took the place of the pain she could not allow herself to feel. Hate flooded through her, filled her with so much demonic energy that she was nearly able to toss the heavy beam off her legs.

Damn you to Hell, Mama.

The top floor of the house caved in upon the ground floor with a sound like cannons blasting.

Damn you, Mama! Damn you!

The first two floors of flaming rubble broke through the already weakened cellar ceiling.

Mama—

PART ONE

Something Wicked This Way Comes...

By the pricking of my thumbs,
Something wicked this way comes.
  Open, locks,
    whoever knocks!

—Shakespeare, *Macbeth*

1

ACROSS the somber gray clouds, lightning followed a jagged course like cracks in a china plate. In the unsheltered courtyard outside Alfred O'Brian's office, the parked cars glimmered briefly with hard-edged reflections of the storm light. The wind gusted, whipping the trees. Rain beat with sudden fury against the three tall office windows, then streamed down the glass, blurring the view beyond.

O'Brian sat with his back to the windows. While thunder reverberated through the low sky and seemed to hammer on the roof of the building, he read the application that Paul and Carol Tracy had just submitted to him.

He's such a neat little man, Carol thought as she watched O'Brian. When he sits very still like that, you'd almost think he was a mannequin.

He was exceedingly well groomed. His carefully combed hair looked as if it had received the attention of a good barber less than an hour ago. His mustache was so expertly trimmed that the halves of it appeared to be perfectly symmetrical. He was wearing a gray suit with trouser creases as tight and straight as blades, and his black shoes gleamed. His fingernails were manicured, and his pink, well-scrubbed hands looked sterile.

When Carol had been introduced to O'Brian less than a week ago, she had thought he was prim, even prissy, and she had been prepared to dislike him. She was quickly won over by his smile, by his gracious manner, and by his sincere desire to help her and Paul.

She glanced at Paul, who was sitting in the chair next to hers, his own tensions betrayed by the angular position of his lean, usually graceful body. He was watching O'Brian intently, but when he sensed that Carol was looking at him, he turned and smiled. His smile was even nicer than O'Brian's, and as usual, Carol's spirits were lifted by the sight of it. He was neither handsome nor ugly, this man she loved; you might even say he was plain, yet his face was enormously appealing because the pleasing, open composition of it contained ample evidence of his gentleness and sensitivity. His hazel eyes were capable of conveying amazingly subtle degrees and mixtures of emotions. Six years ago, at a university symposium entitled "Abnormal Psychology and Modern American Fiction," where Carol had met Paul, the first thing that had drawn her to him had been those warm, expressive eyes, and in the intervening years they had never ceased to intrigue her. Now he winked, and with that wink he seemed to be saying: *Don't worry;*

O'Brian is on our side; the application will be accepted; everything will turn out all right; I love you.

She winked back at him and pretended to be confident, even though she was sure he could see through her brave front.

She wished that she could be certain of winning Mr. O'Brian's approval. She knew she ought to be overflowing with confidence, for there really was no reason why O'Brian would reject them. They were healthy and young. Paul was thirty-five, and she was thirty-one, and those were excellent ages at which to set out upon the adventure they were contemplating. Both of them were successful in their work. They were financially solvent, even prosperous. They were respected in their community. Their marriage was happy and trouble-free, stronger now than at any time in the four years since their wedding. In short, their qualifications for adopting a child were pretty much impeccable, but she worried nonetheless.

She loved children, and she was looking forward to raising one or two of her own. During the past fourteen years—in which she had earned three degrees at three universities and had established herself in her profession—she had postponed many simple pleasures and had skipped others altogether. Getting an education and launching her career had always come first. She had missed too many good parties and had foregone an unremembered number of vacations and getaway weekends. Adopting a child was one pleasure she did not want to postpone any longer.

She had a strong psychological need—almost a *physical* need—to be a mother, to guide and shape children, to give them love and understanding. She was intelligent enough and sufficiently self-aware to

realize that this deep-seated need arose, at least in
part, from her inability to conceive a child of her own
flesh and blood.

The thing we want most, she thought, is always
the thing we cannot have.

She was to blame for her sterility, which was the
result of an unforgivable act of stupidity committed
a long time ago; and of course her culpability made
her condition harder to bear than it would have been
if nature—rather than her own foolishness—had
cursed her with a barren womb. She had been a severely troubled child, for she had been raised by violent, alcoholic parents who had frequently beaten her
and who had dealt out large doses of psychological
torture. By the time she was fifteen, she was a hellion,
engaged in an angry rebellion against her parents and
against the world at large. She hated everyone in those
days, especially herself. In the blackest hours of her
confused and tormented adolescence, she had gotten
pregnant. Frightened, panicky, with no one to turn
to, she tried to conceal her condition by wearing gir-
dles, by binding herself with elastic cloth and tape,
and by eating as lightly as possible to keep her weight
down. Eventually, however, complications arose because of her attempts to hide her pregnancy, and she
nearly died. The baby was born prematurely, but it
was healthy. She had put it up for adoption and hadn't
given it much thought for a couple of years, though
these days she often wondered about the child and
wished she could have kept it somehow. At the time,
the fact that her ordeal had left her sterile did not
depress her, for she didn't think she would ever want
to be pregnant again. But with a lot of help and love
from a child psychologist named Grace Mitowski,

who did charity work among juvenile wards of the court, Carol had turned her life completely around. She had learned to like herself and, years later, had come to regret the thoughtless actions that had left her barren.

Fortunately, she regarded adoption as a more-than-adequate solution to her problem. She was capable of giving as much love to an adopted child as she would have given to her own offspring. She knew she would be a good and caring mother, and she longed to prove it—not to the world but to herself; she never needed to prove anything to anyone but herself, for she was always her own toughest critic.

Mr. O'Brian looked up from the application and smiled. His teeth were exceedingly white. "This looks really fine," he said, indicating the form he had just finished reading. "In fact, it's splendid. Not everyone that applies to us has credentials like these."

"It's kind of you to say so," Paul told him.

O'Brian shook his head. "Not at all. It's simply the truth. Very impressive."

Carol said, "Thank you."

Leaning back in his chair, folding his hands on his stomach, O'Brian said, "I *do* have a couple of questions. I'm sure they're the same ones the recommendations committee will ask me, so I might as well get your responses now and save a lot of back-and-forth later on."

Carol stiffened again.

O'Brian apparently noticed her reaction, for he quickly said, "Oh, it's nothing terribly serious. Really, it isn't. Believe me—I won't be asking you half as many questions as I ask most couples who come to see us."

In spite of O'Brian's assurances, Carol remained tense.

Outside, the storm-dark afternoon sky grew steadily darker as the thunderheads changed color from gray to blue black, thickened, and pressed closer to the earth.

O'Brian swiveled in his chair to face Paul. "Dr. Tracy, would you say you're an overachiever?"

Paul seemed surprised by the question. He blinked and said, "I'm not sure what you mean."

"You *are* the chairman of the department of English at the college, aren't you?"

"Yes. I'm on sabbatical this semester, and the vice-chairman is handling most things for the time being. Otherwise, I've been in charge of the department for the past year and a half."

"Aren't you rather young to hold such a post?"

"Somewhat young," Paul admitted. "But that's no credit to me. You see, it's a thankless position, all work and no glory. My senior colleagues in the department craftily maneuvered me into it so that none of them would be stuck with the job."

"You're being modest."

"No, I'm really not," Paul said. "It's nothing much."

Carol knew that he *was* being modest. The departmental chairmanship was a prized position, an honor. But she understood why Paul was playing it down; he had been unsettled by O'Brian's use of the word *overachiever*. She had been unsettled by it, too. Until this moment she had never thought that an unusually long list of achievements might count *against* them.

Beyond the tall windows, lightning zigzagged

down the sky. The day flickered and, just for a second or two, so did the electric lights in O'Brian's office.

Still addressing Paul, O'Brian said, "You're also an author."

"Yes."

"You've written a very successful textbook for use in American literature courses. You've turned out a dozen monographs on a variety of subjects, and you've done a local history of the county. *And* two children's books, *and* a novel. . . ."

"The novel was about as successful as a horse trying to walk a tightrope," Paul said. "The *New York Times* critic said it was 'a perfect example of academic posturing, stuffed full of themes and symbols, utterly lacking in substance and narrative drive, infused with ivory-tower naivete.'"

O'Brian smiled. "Does every writer memorize his bad reviews?"

"I suppose not. But I have that one engraved on my cerebral cortex because there's an uncomfortable amount of truth in it."

"Are you writing another novel? Is that why you've taken a sabbatical?"

Paul was not surprised by the question. Clearly he now understood what O'Brian was digging for. "Yes, in fact I *am* writing a new novel. This one actually has a plot." He laughed with easy self-deprecation.

"You're also involved in charity work."

"Not much."

"Quite a lot," O'Brian disagreed. "The Children's Hospital Fund, the Community Chest, the student scholarship program at the college—all of that in addition to your regular job and your writing. Yet you don't think you're an overachiever?"

"No, I really don't think I am. The charity work amounts to just a couple of meetings a month. It's no big thing. It's the least I can do, considering my own good fortune." Paul edged forward on his chair. "Maybe you're worried that I won't have time to give to a child, but if that's what's troubling you, then you can put your mind at rest. I'll *make* the time. This adoption is extremely important to us, Mr. O'Brian. We both want a child very badly, and if we are lucky enough to get one, we certainly won't ever neglect it."

"Oh, I'm sure you won't," O'Brian said quickly, raising his hands placatingly. "That isn't at all what I meant to imply. Oh, certainly not. I'm on *your* side in this matter. I mean that very sincerely." He swiveled to face Carol. "Dr. Tracy—the *other* Dr. Tracy— what about you? Do you consider yourself an over-achiever?"

Lightning slashed through the panoply of clouds again, nearer this time than before; it seemed to strike the ground no more than two blocks away. The ensuing crash of thunder rattled the tall windows.

Carol used the interruption provided by the thunderclap to consider her response, and she decided that O'Brian would appreciate forthrightness more than modesty. "Yes. I'd say I'm an overachiever. I'm involved in two of the three charities that Paul has his hand in. And I know I'm a bit young to have established a psychiatric practice as successful as mine is. I'm also a guest lecturer at the college on a fairly regular basis. And I'm doing post-doctoral research on autistic children. During the summer I manage to keep a little vegetable garden going, and I do some needlepoint in the winter months, and I even brush my teeth *three* times a day, every day, without fail."

O'Brian laughed. "Three times a day, huh? Oh, you're most *definitely* an overachiever."

The warmth of his laughter reassured Carol, and with renewed confidence she said, "I believe I understand what you're concerned about. You're wondering if Paul and I might expect too much of our child."

"Exactly," O'Brian said. He noticed a speck of lint on his coat sleeve and plucked it off. "Parents who are overachievers tend to push their kids too hard, too fast, too soon."

Paul said, "That's a problem that arises only when parents are unaware of the danger. Even if Carol and I are overachievers—which *I'm* not prepared to admit just yet—we wouldn't pressure our kids to do more than they were capable of doing. Each of us has to find his own pace in life. Carol and I realize that a child should be guided, not hammered into a mold."

"Of course," Carol said.

O'Brian appeared to be pleased. "I knew you'd say that—or something very like it."

Lightning flashed again. This time it seemed to strike even closer than before, only a block away. Thunder cracked, then cracked again. The overhead lights dimmed, fluttered, reluctantly came back to full power.

"In my psychiatric practice, I deal with a wide variety of patients who have all kinds of problems," Carol told O'Brian, "but I specialize in the mental disorders and emotional disturbances of children and adolescents. Sixty or seventy percent of my patients are seventeen or younger. I've treated several kids who've suffered serious psychological damage at the hands of parents who were too demanding, who pushed them too hard in their schoolwork, in every aspect of their intellectual and personal development. I've seen the wounded ones, Mr. O'Brian, and I've nursed them as best I could, and because of those experiences, I couldn't possibly turn around and do to my children what I've seen some parents do to theirs. Not that I won't make mistakes. I'm sure I will. My full share of them. But the one that you mentioned won't be among them."

"That's valid," O'Brian said, nodding. "Valid and very well put. I'm sure that when I tell the recommendations committee what you've just said, they'll be quite satisfied on this point." He spotten another tiny speck on his sleeve and removed it, frowning as if it were not merely lint, but offal. "Another question they're bound to ask: Suppose the child you adopt turns out to be not only an underachiever but . . . well . . . basically less intelligent than either of you. For parents as oriented toward an intellectual life as you are, wouldn't you be somewhat frustrated with a child of just average—or possibly slightly below average—intelligence?"

"Well, even if we were capable of having a child of our own," Paul said, "there wouldn't be any guarantee that he'd be a prodigy or anything of that sort. But if he was . . . slow . . . we'd still love him. Of course we would. And the same goes for any child we might adopt."

To O'Brian, Carol said, "I think you've got too high an opinion of us. Neither of us is a *genius*, for heaven's sake! We've gotten as far as we have primarily through hard work and perseverence, not because we were exceptionally bright. I wish it *had* come that easy, but it didn't."

"Besides," Paul said, "you don't love a person merely because he's intelligent. It's his entire personality that counts, the whole package, and a lot of factors contribute to that package, a great many things other than just intellect."

"Good," O'Brian said. "I'm glad to hear you feel that way. The committee will respond well to that answer, too."

For the past few seconds, Carol had been aware of the distant wail of sirens. Fire engines. Now they were not as distant as they had been; they were rapidly growing nearer, louder.

"I think maybe one of those last two bolts of lightning caused some real damage when it touched down," Paul said.

O'Brian swung his chair around toward the center window, which was directly behind his desk. "It *did* sound as if it struck nearby."

Carol looked at each of the three windows, but she couldn't see any smoke rising from behind the nearest rooftops. Then again, the view was blurred and visibility was reduced by the water-spotted panes of glass and by the curtains of mist and gray rain that wavered and whipped and billowed beyond the glass.

The sirens swelled.

"More than one truck," O'Brian said.

The fire engines were right outside the office for a moment—at least two trucks, perhaps three—and then they passed, heading into the next block.

O'Brian pushed up from his chair and stepped to the window.

As the first sirens dwindled just a little, new ones shrieked in the street behind them.

"Must be serious," Paul said. "Sounds as if at least two engine companies are responding."

"I see smoke," O'Brian said.

Paul rose from his chair and moved toward the windows to get a better look.

Something's wrong here.

That thought snapped into Carol's mind, startling her as if a whip had cracked in front of her face. A powerful, inexplicable current of panic surged through her, electrified her. She gripped the arms of her chair so tightly that one of her fingernails broke.

Something . . . is . . . wrong . . . very wrong . . .

Suddenly the air was oppressively heavy—hot, *thick*, as if it were not air at all but a bitter and poisonous gas of some kind. She tried to breathe, couldn't. There was an invisible, crushing weight on her chest.

Get away from the windows!

She tried to shout that warning, but panic had shortcircuited her voice. Paul and O'Brian were at different windows, but they both had their backs to her, so that neither of them could see she had been gripped by sudden, immobilizing fear.

Fear of what? she demanded of herself. What in the name of God am I so scared of?

She struggled against the unreasonable terror that had locked her muscles and joints. She started to get up from the chair, and that was when it happened.

A murderous barrage of lightning crashed like a volley of mortar fire, seven or eight tremendous bolts, perhaps more than that—she didn't count them, couldn't count them—one right after the other, without a significant pause between them, each fierce boom overlapping the ones before and after it, yet each clearly louder than its predecessors, so loud that they made her teeth and bones vibrate, each bolt smashing down discernibly closer to the building than had the bolt before it, closer to the seven-foot-high windows—the gleaming, flashing, rattling, now-black, now-milky, now-shining, now-blank, now-silvery, now-coppery windows. . . .

The sharp bursts of purple-white light produced a series of jerky, stroboscopic images that were burned forever into Carol's memory: Paul and O'Brian standing there, silhouetted against the natural fireworks, looking small and vulnerable; outside, the rain descending in an illusion of hesitation; wind-lashed trees heaving in a strobe-choppy rage; lightning blasting into one of those trees, a big maple, and then an ominous dark shape rising from the midst of the explosion, a torpedolike thing, spinning straight toward the center window (all of this transpiring in only a second or two, but given a queer, slow-motion quality by the flickering lightning and, after a moment, by the overhead electric light as well, which began to flicker, too); O'Brian throwing one arm up in front of his face in what appeared to be half a dozen disconnected movements; Paul turning toward O'Brian and reaching for him, both men like figures on a motion picture screen when the film slips and stutters in the projector; O'Brian lurching sideways; Paul seizing him by a coat sleeve, pulling him back and down toward safety (only a fraction of a second after the lightning splintered the maple); a huge tree limb bursting through the center window even as Paul was pulling O'Brian out of the way; one leafy branch sweeping

across O'Brian's head, ripping his glasses loose, tossing them into the air—his face, Carol thought, his
eyes!—and then Paul and O'Brian falling to the floor,
out of sight; the enormous limb of the shattered maple
slamming down on top of O'Brian's desk in a spray
of water, glass, broken mullions, and smoking chips
of bark; the legs of the desk cracking and collapsing
under the brutal impact of the ruined tree.

Carol found herself on the floor, beside her overturned chair. She couldn't remember falling.

The fluorescent tubes blinked off, stayed off.

She was lying on her stomach, one cheek pressed
to the floor, staring in shock at the shards of glass and
the torn maple leaves that littered the carpet. As lightning continued to stab down from the turbulent sky,
wind roared through the missing window and stirred
some of the loose leaves into a frantic, dervishlike
dance; accompanied by the cacophonous music of the
storm, they whirled and capered across the office,
toward a row of green filing cabinets. A calendar
flapped off the wall and swooped around on wings
of January and December, darting and soaring and
kiting as if it were a bat. Two paintings rattled on
their wire hangers, trying to tear themselves free.
Papers were everywhere—stationery, forms, small
sheets from a note pad, bulletins, a newspaper—all
rustling and skipping this way and that, floating up,
diving down, bunching together and slithering along
the floor with a snakelike hiss.

Carol had the eerie feeling that all of the movement
in the room was not solely the result of the wind, that
some of it was caused by a *...presence*. Something
threatening. A bad poltergeist. Demonic spirits seemed

to be at work in the office, flexing their occult muscles, knocking things off the walls, briefly taking up residence in a body composed only of leaves and rumpled sheets of newsprint.

That was a crazy idea, not at all the sort of thing she would ordinarily think of. She was surprised and disconcerted by a thrill of superstitious fear that coursed through her.

Lightning flared again. And again.

Wincing at the painfully sharp sound, wondering if lightning could get into a room through an open window, she put her arms over her head, for what little protection they provided.

Her heart was pounding, and her mouth was dry.

She thought about Paul, and her heartbeat grew even more frantic. He was over by the windows, on the far side of the desk, out of sight, under some of the maple tree's branches. She didn't think he was dead. He hadn't been directly in the path of the tree. O'Brian might be dead, yes, depending on how that small branch had struck his head, depending on whether he had been lucky or not, because maybe a pointed twig had been driven deep into his eye and his brain when his glasses had been knocked off, but Paul was surely alive. Surely. Nevertheless, he could be seriously injured, bleeding....

Carol started to push herself up onto her hands and knees, anxious to find Paul and give him any first aid he might need. But another bolt of blinding, ear-shattering lightning spent itself just outside the building, and fear turned her muscles into wet rags. She didn't even have the strength to crawl, and she was infuriated by her weakness, for she had always been proud of her strength, determination, and unflagging willpower. Cursing herself, she slumped back to the floor.

Something's trying to stop us from adopting a baby.

That incredible thought struck her with the same cold, hard force as had the forewarning of the window's implosion, which had come to her an instant before the impossible barrage of lightning had blasted into the courtyard.

Something's trying to stop us from adopting a baby.

No. That was ridiculous. The storm, the lightning—they were nothing more than acts of nature. They hadn't been directed against Mr. O'Brian just because he was going to help them adopt a child. Absurd.

Oh, yeah? she thought as the deafening thunder and the unholy light of the storm filled the room. Acts of nature, huh? When have you ever seen lightning like *this* before?

She hugged the floor, shaking, cold, more afraid than she had been since she was a little girl. She tried to tell herself that it was only the lightning that she was afraid of, for that was very much a legitimate, rational fear, but she knew she was lying. It was *not* just the lightning that terrified her. In fact, that was the least of it. There was something else, something she couldn't identify, something formless and nameless in the room, and the very presence of it, whatever the hell it was, pushed a panic button deep inside her, on a sub-subconscious, primitive level; this fear was gut-deep, instinctive.

A dervish of windblown leaves and papers whirled across the floor, directly toward her. It was a big one: a column about two feet in diameter, five or six feet high, composed of a hundred or more pieces of this and that. It stopped very near her, writhing, churning, hissing, changing shape, glimmering silver-dark in the flashing storm light, and she felt threatened by it. As she stared up at the whirlwind, she had the mad notion that it was staring down at her. After a moment it moved off to the left a few feet, then returned, paused in front of her again, hesitated, then scurried busily to the right, but came back once more, looming above her as if it were trying to make up its mind whether or not to pounce and tear her to shreds and sweep her up along with the leaves, newspaper pages, envelopes, and other flotsam by which it defined itself.

It's nothing more than a whirlwind of lifeless junk! she told herself angrily.

The wind-shaped phantom moved away from her.

See? she told herself scornfully. Just lifeless junk. What's wrong with me? Am I losing my mind?

She recalled the old axiom that was supposed to provide comfort in moments like this: If you think you're going mad, then you must be completely sane, for a lunatic never has doubts about his sanity. As a psychiatrist, she knew that hoary bit of wisdom was an oversimplification of complex psychological principles, but in essence it was true. So she must be sane.

Nevertheless, that frightening, irrational thought came to her again, unbidden, unwanted: *Something's trying to stop us from adopting a baby.*

If the maelstrom in which she lay was not an act of nature, then what *was* it? Was she to believe that the lightning had been sent with the conscious intent of transforming Mr. O'Brian into a smoking heap of charred flesh? That was a fruitcake notion, for sure.

Who could use lightning as if it were a pistol? God? God wasn't sitting up in Heaven, aiming at Mr. O'Brian, popping away at him with lightning bolts, just to screw up the adoption process for Carol and Paul Tracy. The Devil? Blasting away at poor Mr. O'Brian from the depths of Hell? That *was* a looney idea. *Jesus!*

She wasn't even sure she believed in God, but she knew she definitely did not believe in the Devil.

Another window imploded, showering glass over her.

Then the lightning stopped.

The thunder decreased from a roar to a rumble, fading like the noise of a passing freight train.

There was a stench of ozone.

The wind was still pouring in through the broken windows, but apparently with less force than it had exerted a moment ago, for the whirling columns of leaves and papers subsided to the floor, where they lay in piles, fluttering and quivering as if exhausted.

Something . . .

Something . . .

Something's trying to stop us from—

She clamped off that unwanted thought as though it were a spurting artery. She was an educated woman, dammit. She prided herself on her levelheadedness and common sense. She couldn't permit herself to succumb to these disturbing, uncharacteristic, utterly superstitious fears.

Freaky weather—that was the explanation for the lightning. Freaky weather. You read about such things in the newspapers every once in a while. A half an inch of snow in Beverly Hills. An eighty-degree day in the middle of an otherwise frigid Minnesota winter.

Rain falling briefly from an apparently cloudless blue sky. Although a lightning strike of this magnitude and intensity was undoubtedly a rare occurrence, it probably had happened before, sometime, somewhere, probably more than once. Of course it had. Of course. In fact, if you picked up one of those popular books in which the authors compiled all kinds of world records, and if you turned to the chapter on weather, and if you looked for a subsection entitled "Lightning," you would most likely find an impressive list of other serial lightning strikes that would put this one to shame. Freaky weather. That's what it was. That's *all* it was. Nothing stranger than that, nothing worse.

For the time being, at least, Carol managed to put aside all thoughts of demons and ghosts and malign poltergeists and other such claptrap.

In the relative quiet that followed in the wake of the fast-diminishing thunder, she felt her strength returning. She pushed up from the floor, onto her knees. With the clinking sound of mildly disturbed wind chimes, pieces of glass fell from her gray skirt and green blouse; she wasn't cut or even scratched. She was a bit dazed, however, and for a moment the floor appeared to roll sickeningly from side to side, as if this were a stateroom aboard a ship.

In the office next door, a woman began to cry hysterically. There were shouts of alarm, and someone began calling for Mr. O'Brian. No one had yet burst into the office to see what had happened, which meant that only a second or two had elapsed since the lightning had stopped, although it seemed to Carol as if a minute or two had passed.

Over by the windows, someone groaned softly.

"Paul?" she said.

If there was an answer, it was drowned out by a sudden gust of wind that briefly stirred the papers and leaves again.

She recalled the way that branch had whipped across O'Brian's head, and she shuddered. But Paul hadn't been touched. The tree had missed him. Hadn't it?

"Paul!"

With renewed fear, she got to her feet and moved quickly around the desk, stepping over splintered maple branches and an overturned wastebasket.

2

THAT Wednesday afternoon, following a lunch of Campbell's vegetable soup and a grilled cheese sandwich, Grace Mitowski went into her study and curled up on the sofa to sleep for an hour or so. She never napped in the bedroom because that formalized it somehow, and though she had been taking naps three or four days a week for the past year, she still had not reconciled herself to the fact that she needed a midday rest. To her way of thinking, naps were for children and for old, used-up, burnt-out people. She wasn't in her childhood any more—neither the first nor the second, thank you—and although she *was* old, she certainly wasn't used up or burnt out. Being in bed in the middle of the day made her feel lazy, and she couldn't abide laziness in anyone, especially not in herself. Therefore, she took naps on the study sofa, with her back to the shuttered windows, lulled by the monotonous ticking of the mantel clock.

At seventy, Grace was still as *mentally* agile and energetic as she had ever been. Her gray matter hadn't begun to deteriorate at all; it was only her treacherous body that caused her grief and frustration. She had a touch of arthritis in her hands, and when the humidity was high—as it was today—she also suffered from a dull but unrelenting ache of bursitis in her shoulders. Although she did all of the exercises that her doctor recommended, and although she walked two miles every morning, she found it increasingly difficult to maintain her muscle tone. From the time she was a young girl, throughout most of her life, she had been in love with books, and she had been able to read all morning, all afternoon, and most of the evening without eyestrain; nowadays, usually after only a couple of hours of reading, her eyes felt grainy and hot. She regarded each of her infirmities with extreme indignation, and she struggled against them, even though she knew this was a war she was destined to lose.

That Wednesday afternoon she took a break from the battle, a brief period of R and R. Two minutes after she stretched out on the sofa, she was asleep.

Grace did not dream often, and she was even less often plagued by *bad* dreams. But Wednesday afternoon, in the book-lined study, her sleep was continuously disturbed by nightmares. Several times she stirred, came half awake, and heard herself gasping in panic. Once, drifting up from some hideous and threatening vision, she heard her own voice crying out wordlessly in terror, and she realized she was thrashing on the couch, twisting and torturing her aching shoulders. She tried to come fully awake, but she could not; something in the dream, something dark and menacing, reached up with icy, clammy hands and pulled her down into deep sleep again, down and down, all the way down into a lightless place where an unnameable creature gibbered and muttered and chuckled in a mucous-wet voice.

An hour later, when she finally woke up and managed to cast off the clutching dream, she was standing in the middle of the shadow-shrouded room, several steps away from the sofa, but she had no memory of getting to her feet. She was shaking, sheathed in sweat.

—*I've got to tell Carol Tracy.*
—*Tell her what?*
—*Warn her.*
—*Warn her about what?*
—*It's coming. Oh, God . . .*
—*What's coming?*
—*Just like in the dream.*
—*What about the dream?*

Already her memory of the nightmare had begun to dissolve; only fragments of it remained with her, and each of those disassociated images was evaporating as if it were a splinter of dry ice. All she could remember was that Carol had been a part of it, and had been in awful danger. And somehow she knew that the dream had been more than just an ordinary dream. . . .

As the nightmare receded, Grace became uncomfortably aware of how gloomy the study was. Before taking her nap, she had switched off the lamps. The shutters were all closed, and only thin blades of light were visible between the wooden slats. She had the irrational but unshakable feeling that something had followed her up from the dream, something vicious and evil that had undergone a magical metamorphosis from a creature of the imagination into one composed of solid flesh, something that was now crouched in a corner, watching, waiting.

—*Stop it!*

—*But the dream was . . .*

—*Only a dream.*

Along the edges of the shutters, the taut threads of light abruptly brightened, then dimmed, then grew bright again as lightning flashed outside. A roof-rattling crash of thunder quickly followed, and more lightning, too, an unbelievable amount of it, one blue-white explosion after another, so that for at least half a minute the cracks in the shutters looked like sputtering electrical wires, white-hot with sparking current.

Still drugged with sleep and slightly confused, Grace stood in the middle of the unlighted room, rocking from side to side, listening to the thunder and the wind, watching the intense pulse of lightning. The extreme violence of the storm seemed unreal, and she concluded that she was still under the influence of the dream, misinterpreting what she was seeing. It couldn't possibly be as savage outside as it appeared to be.

"Grace . . ."

She thought she heard something call to her from over by the tallest set of bookshelves, directly behind her. Judging from its slurred, distorted pronunciation of her name, its mouth was severely malformed.

There's nothing behind me! Nothing.

Nevertheless, she did not turn around.

When the lightning finally stopped and the long-sustained crescendo of thunder subsided, the air seemed thicker than it had been a minute ago. She had difficulty breathing. The room was darker, too.

"Grace..."

A confining mantle of claustrophobia settled over her. The dimly visible walls appeared to ripple and move closer, as if the chamber might shrink around her until it was precisely the size and shape of a coffin.

"Grace..."

She stumbled to the nearest window, banging her hip against the desk, nearly tripping over a lamp cord. She fumbled with the lever on the shutters, her fingers stiff and unresponsive. At last the slats opened wide; gray but welcome light poured into the study, forcing her to squint but gladdening her as well. She leaned against the shutters and stared out at the cloud-plated sky, resisting the insane urge to look over her shoulder to see if there really was something monstrous lurking there with a hungry grin on its face. She drew deep, gasping breaths, as if the daylight itself—rather than the air—sustained her.

Grace's house was atop a small knoll, at the end of a quiet street, sheltered by several large pine trees and by one enormous weeping willow; from her study window she could see the rain-swollen Susquehanna a couple of miles away. Harrisburg, the state capital, huddled solemnly, drearily along the river's banks. The clouds hung low over the city, trailing bedraggled beards of mist that obscured the upper floors of the tallest buildings.

When she'd blinked the last grains of sleep out of her eyes, when her nerves had stopped jangling, she turned around and surveyed the room. A quiver of relief swept through her, unknotting her muscles.

She was alone.

With the storm temporarily quiet, she could hear the mantel clock again. It was the only sound.

Hell, yes, you're alone, she told herself scornfully. What did you expect? A green goblin with three eyes and a mouthful of sharp teeth? You better watch yourself, Grace Louise Mitowski, or you'll wind up in a rest home, sitting all day in a rocking chair, happily chatting with ghosts, while smiling nurses wipe drool off your chin.

Having led an active life of the mind for so many years, she worried more about creeping senility than about anything else. She knew she was as sharp and alert as she had ever been. But what about tomorrow and the day after? Because of her medical training, and because she had kept up with her professional reading even after closing down her psychiatric practice, she was up to date on all the latest findings about senility, and she knew that only fifteen percent of all elderly people suffered from it. She also knew that more than half of those cases were treatable with proper nutrition and exercise. She knew her chances of becoming mentally incapacitated were small, only about one in eighteen. Nevertheless, although she was conscious of her excessive sensitivity regarding the subject, she still worried. Consequently, she was understandably disturbed by this uncharacteristic notion that something had been in the study with her a few moments ago, something hostile and . . . supernatural. As a lifelong skeptic with little or no patience for astrologers and psychics and their ilk, she could not justify even a fleeting belief in such superstitious non-

sense; to her way of thinking, beliefs of that nature
were . . . well . . . feebleminded.

But good, sweet God, what a nightmare that had
been!

She had never before experienced a dream even
one-tenth as bad as that one. Although the grisly
details had completely faded away, she could still
clearly remember the mood of it—the terror, the gut-
wrenching horror that had permeated every nasty image, every ticking sound.

She shivered.

The sweat that the dream had squeezed out of her
was beginning to feel like a thin glaze of ice on her
skin.

The only other thing she remembered from the
nightmare was Carol. Screaming. Crying for help.

Until now, none of Grace's infrequent dreams had
included Carol, and there was a temptation to view
her appearance in this one with alarm, to see it as an
omen. But of course it wasn't surprising that Carol
should eventually have a role in one of Grace's
dreams, for the loved-one-in-danger theme was common in nightmares. Any psychologist would attest to
that, and Grace was a psychologist, a good one, although she was entering her third year of retirement.
She cared deeply about Carol. If she'd had a child of
her own, she couldn't have loved it any more than she
loved Carol.

She had first met the girl sixteen years ago, when
Carol had been an angry, obstinate, obstreperous fifteen-year-old delinquent who had recently given birth
to a baby that had nearly killed her, and who, subsequent to that traumatic episode, had been remanded

to a juvenile detention facility for possession of marijuana and for a host of other offenses. In those days, in addition to a private psychiatric practice, Grace had performed eight hours a week of free service to assist the overworked counseling staff at the reform school in which Carol was held. Carol was incorrigible, determined to kick you in the teeth if you smiled at her, but even then her intelligence and innate goodness were there, to be seen by anyone who looked closely enough, beneath the rough exterior. Grace had taken a very close look indeed, and had been intrigued, impressed. The girl's obsessively foul language, her vicious temper, and her amoral pose had been nothing more than defense mechanisms, shields with which she protected herself from the physical and psychological abuse dished out by her parents.

As Grace gradually unearthed the horrendous story of Carol's monstrous home life, she became convinced that reform school was the wrong place for the girl. She used her influence with the court to get Carol permanently removed from the custody of her parents. Later, she arranged to serve as Carol's foster parent. She had watched the girl respond to love and guidance, had watched her grow from a brooding, self-centered, self-destructive teenager into a warm, self-assured, admirable young woman with hopes and dreams, a woman of character, a sensitive woman. Playing a part in that exciting transformation had been perhaps the most satisfying thing that Grace had ever done.

The only regret she had about her relationship with Carol was the role she had played in putting the baby up for adoption. But there had been no reasonable alternative. Carol simply hadn't been financially or emotionally or mentally capable of providing for the infant. With that responsibility to attend to, she would never have had an opportunity to grow and change. She would have been miserable all her life, and she would have made her child miserable, too. Unfortunately, even now, sixteen years later, Carol felt guilty about giving her baby away. Her guilt became overpowering on each anniversary of the child's birth. On that black day, Carol sank into a deep depression and became uncharacteristically uncommunicative. The excessive anguish that she suffered on that one day was evidence of the deep-seated, abiding guilt that she carried with her, to a lesser degree, during the rest of the year. Grace wished she had foreseen this reaction, wished she had done more to assuage Carol's guilt.

I'm a psychologist, after all, she thought. I should have anticipated it.

Perhaps when Carol and Paul adopted someone else's child, Carol would feel that the scales had at last been balanced. The adoption might relieve some of her guilt, in time.

Grace hoped it would. She loved Carol like a daughter and wanted only the best for her.

And of course she couldn't bear the thought of losing Carol. Therefore, Carol's appearance in a nightmare wasn't the least bit mysterious. It was certainly *not* an omen.

Clammy with stale sweat, Grace turned to the study window again, seeking warmth and light, but the day was ashen, chilly, forbidding. Wind pressed on the glass, soughed softly under the eaves one floor above.

In the city, near the river, a roiling column of

smoke rose into the rain and mist. She had not noticed it a minute ago, but it must have been there; it was too much smoke to have appeared in only a few seconds. Even from this distance, she could see a glint of fire at the base of the dark column.

She wondered if lightning had done the dirty work. She recalled the storm flashing and roaring with extraordinary power in those first seconds after she had awakened. At the time, groggy and bleary-eyed, she had thought her sleep-dulled senses were misleading her and that the extreme violence of the lightning was largely illusory or even imaginary. Could that incredible, destructive barrage have been real after all?

She glanced at her wristwatch.

Her favorite radio station would carry its hourly newscast in less than ten minutes. Maybe there would be a story about the fire and the lightning.

After she'd straightened the throw pillows on the sofa, she stepped out of the study and spotted Aristophanes at the far end of the downstairs hall, near the front door. He was sitting up straight and tall, his tail curled forward and across his front paws, his head held high, as if he were saying, "A Siamese cat is the very best thing on earth, and I am an exceedingly handsome example of the species, and don't you dare forget it."

Grace held one hand toward him, rapidly rubbing her thumb against her forefinger. "Kitty-kitty-kitty."

Aristophanes didn't move.

"Kitty-kitty-kitty. Come here, Ari. Come on, baby."

Aristophanes got up and went through the archway on his left, into the dark living room.

"Stubborn damn cat," she said affectionately.

She went into the downstairs bathroom and washed her face and combed her hair. The mundane task of grooming herself took her mind off the nightmare. Gradually, she began to relax. Her eyes were watery and bloodshot. She rinsed them out with a few drops of Murine.

When she came out of the bathroom, Aristophanes was sitting in the hallway again, watching her.

"Kitty-kitty-kitty," she coaxed.

He stared unblinkingly.

"Kitty-kitty-kitty."

Aristophanes rose to his feet, cocked his head, and examined her with curious, shining eyes. When she took a step toward him, he turned and quickly slunk away, casting one backward glance, then disappearing into the living room again.

"Okay," Grace said. "Okay, buster. Have it your way. Snub me if you want. But just see if there's any Meow Mix in *your* bowl tonight."

In the kitchen she snapped on the lights, then the radio. The station came in clearly enough, though there was a continuous crackle of storm-generated static.

While she listened to tales of economic crises and breathless accounts of airplane hijackings and rumors of war, Grace put a clean paper filter in the coffee machine, filled the brewing basket with drip-ground Colombian, and added half a spoonful of chicory. The story of the fire came at the end of the newscast, and it was only a sketchy bulletin. The reporter knew nothing more than that lightning had struck a couple of buildings in the heart of the city and that one of them, a church, was afire. He promised more details on the half hour.

When the coffee was ready, Grace poured some for herself. She took her mug to the small table by the kitchen's only window, pulled out a chair, and sat down.

In the backyard, the myriad roses—red, pink, orange, white, yellow—looked preternaturally bright, almost phosphorescent, against the cinereous backdrop of the rain.

Two psychology journals had arrived in the morning mail. Grace opened one of them with pleasant anticipation.

Halfway through an article about new findings in criminal psychology, as she finished her first mug of coffee, there was a pause between songs on the radio, a few seconds of dead air, and in that brief quietude, she heard furtive movement behind her. She turned in her chair and saw Aristophanes.

"Come to apologize?" she asked.

Then she realized that he appeared to have been sneaking up on her, and that now, confronted, he was frozen; every lithe muscle in his small body was spring-taut, and the fur bristled along his arched back.

"Ari? What's wrong, you silly cat?"

He whirled and ran out of the kitchen.

3

CAROL sat in a chrome chair with shiny black vinyl cushions, and she slowly sipped whiskey from a paper cup.

Paul slumped in the chair next to hers. He didn't sip his whiskey; he gulped the stuff. It was an excellent bourbon, Jack Daniel's Black Label, thoughtfully provided by an attorney named Marvin Kwicker, who had offices down the hall from Alfred O'Brian and who realized that a restorative was urgently needed. Pouring bourbon for Carol, Marvin had said, "Kwicker with liquor," which he had probably said ten thousand times before, but he still enjoyed his own joke. "Kwicker with liquor," he repeated when dispensing a double shot to Paul. Although Paul wasn't much of a drinker, he needed every drop that the attorney gave him. His hands were still shaking.

The reception lounge that served O'Brian's office was not large, but most of the people who worked on the same floor had congregated here to talk about the lightning that had shaken the building, to marvel that the place hadn't caught fire, to express surprise that the electric power had been restored so quickly, and to wait their turns for a peek at the rubble and ruin in O'Brian's inner sanctum. The resultant roar of conversation did nothing to soothe Paul's nerves.

Every thirty seconds or so, a bleached blonde with a shrill voice repeated the same words of amazement: "I can't believe nobody got killed in all that! I can't believe *nobody* got killed." Each time she spoke, regardless of where she was in the room, her voice carried over the din and made Paul wince. "I can't believe *nobody* got killed." She sounded somewhat disappointed.

Alfred O'Brian was sitting at the reception desk. His secretary, a prim-looking woman whose hair was drawn back in a tight bun, was trying to apply Merthiolate to half a dozen scratches on her boss's face, but O'Brian seemed more concerned about the condition of his suit than he was about himself. He plucked and brushed at the dirt, lint, and small fragments of tree bark that clung to his jacket.

Paul finished his whiskey and looked at Carol. She was still badly shaken. Contrasted with her glossy dark hair, her face was very pale.

Apparently, she saw the concern in his eyes, for she took his hand, squeezed it, and smiled reassuringly. However, the smile didn't set well on her lips; it was tremulous.

He leaned close to her, so that she could hear him

above the excited chatter of the others. "Ready to get out of here?"

She nodded.

Over by the window, a young executive type raised his voice. "Hey! Hey, everybody! Better look sharp. The TV news people just drove up to the front door."

"If we get trapped by reporters," Carol said, "we'll be here an hour or more."

They left without saying goodbye to O'Brian. In the hall, as they headed toward a side entrance, they slipped into their raincoats. Outside, Paul opened his umbrella and put one arm around Carol's waist. They hurried across the slippery macadam parking lot, stepping gingerly around huge puddles. The gusting wind was chilly for early September, and it kept changing direction until it finally got under the umbrella and turned it inside out. The cold, wind-driven rain was falling so hard that it stung Paul's face. By the time they reached the car, their hair was plastered to their heads, and a lot of water had found its way down the backs of their necks, under the collars of their coats.

Paul half expected the Pontiac to be lightning-damaged, but it was just as they had left it. The engine turned over without protest.

Leaving the parking lot, he started to turn left but put his foot on the brake pedal when he saw that the street was sealed off by police cars and fire trucks just half a block away. The church was still ablaze, in spite of the pouring rain and in defiance of the big streams of water that the firemen directed onto it. Black smoke billowed into the gray day, and behind the blasted windows, flames spurted and churned. Clearly, the church was going to be a total loss.

He turned right, instead, and drove home through rain-choked streets, where the gutters overflowed and where every depression in the pavement had been transformed into a treacherous lake that had to be negotiated with utmost caution to avoid drowning the engine and stalling out.

Carol slouched in her seat and huddled against the passenger-side door, hugging herself. Although the heater was on, she was obviously cold.

Paul realized his teeth were chattering.

The trip home took ten minutes, and during that time neither of them said a word. The only sounds were the whispery hiss of the tires on the wet pavement and the metronomic thump of the windshield wipers. The silence was not uncomfortable or strained, but there was a peculiar intensity about it, an aura of tremendous, pent-up energy. Paul had the feeling that if he *did* speak, the surprise would send Carol straight through the roof of the car.

They lived in a Tudor-style house, which they had painstakingly restored, and as always, the sight of it—the stone walk, the big oak doors framed by carriage lamps, the leaded-glass windows, the gabled roofline—pleased Paul and gave him the warm feeling that this was where he belonged. The automatic garage door rolled up, and he pulled the Pontiac inside, next to Carol's red Volkswagen Rabbit.

In the house, they maintained their silence.

Paul's hair was wet, and the legs of his trousers clung damply to him, and the back of his shirt was still soaked. He figured he was going to come down with a nasty cold if he didn't get into some dry clothes right away. Apparently, Carol had the same thought, and they went straight upstairs to the master bedroom.

She opened the closet doors, and he switched on a bedside lamp. Shivering, they stripped out of their wet clothes.

When they were nearly undressed, they glanced at each other. Their eyes locked.

Still, they didn't speak. They didn't need to.

He took her in his arms, and they kissed lightly at first, tenderly. Her mouth was warm and soft and vaguely flavored with whiskey.

She clutched him, pulled him closer, her fingertips digging into the muscles of his back. She pushed her mouth hard against his, scraped his lip with her teeth, thrust her tongue deep, and abruptly their kisses grew hot, demanding.

Something seemed to snap in him, and in her, too, for their desire was suddenly marked by animal urgency. They responded to each other in a hungry, almost frenzied fashion, hastily casting off the last of their clothes, pawing at each other, squeezing, stroking. She nipped his shoulder with her teeth. He gripped her buttocks and kneaded them with uncharacteristic crudity, but she didn't wince or try to pull away; indeed, she pressed even more insistently against him, rubbing her breasts over his chest and grinding her hips against his. The soft whimpers that escaped from her were not sounds of pain; they clearly expressed her eagerness and need. In bed, his energy was manic, and his staying power amazed him. He was insatiable, and so was she. They thrust and thrashed and flexed and tensed in perfect harmony, as if they were not only joined but *fused*, as if they were a single organism, shaken by only one set of stimuli instead of two. Every vestige of civilization slipped from them, and for a long while the only noises they made were animal sounds: panting; groaning; throaty grunts of pleasure; short, sharp cries of excitement. At last Carol uttered the first word to pass between them since they had left O'Brian's office: "Yes." And again, arching her slender, graceful body, tossing her head from side to side on the pillow: "Yes, yes!" It was not merely an orgasm to which she was saying yes, for she'd already had a couple of those and had announced them with only ragged breathing and soft mewling. She was saying yes to life, yes to the fact that she still existed and was not just a charred and oozing lump of unanimated flesh, yes to the miraculous fact that they had both survived the lightning and the deadly, splintered branches of the toppling maple tree. Their unrestrained, fiercely passionate coupling was a slap in Death's face, a not wholly rational but nevertheless satisfying denial of the grim specter's very existence. Paul repeated the word as if chanting an incantation—"Yes, yes, yes!"—as he emptied himself into her a second time, and it seemed as though his fear of death spurted out of him along with his seed.

Spent, they stretched out on their backs, side by side on the disheveled bed. For a long time they listened to the rain on the roof and to the persistent thunder, which was no longer loud enough to rattle the windows.

Carol lay with her eyes closed, her face completely relaxed. Paul studied her, and, as he had done on countless other occasions during the past four years, he wondered why she had ever consented to marry him. She was beautiful. He was not. Anyone putting together a dictionary could do worse than to use a picture of his face as the sole definition of the word *plain.* He had once jokingly expressed a similar opinion of his physical appearance, and Carol had been angry with him for talking about himself that way. But it was true, and it didn't really matter to him that he was not Burt Reynolds, just so long as Carol didn't notice the difference. It was not only his plainness of which she seemed unaware; she could not comprehend her own beauty, and she insisted *she* was actually rather plain, or at least no more than "a little bit pretty, no, not even pretty, just sort of cute, but kind of funny-looking cute." Her dark hair—even now, when it was matted and curled by rain and sweat—was thick, glossy, lovely. Her skin was flawless, and her cheekbones were so well sculpted that it was difficult to believe the clumsy hand of nature could have done the job. Carol was the kind of woman you saw on the arm of a tall, bronzed Adonis, not with the likes of Paul Tracy. Yet here she was, and he was grateful to have her beside him. He never ceased to be surprised that they were compatible in every respect—mentally, emotionally, physically.

Now, as rain began to beat on the roof and windows with renewed force, Carol sensed that he was staring at her, and she opened her eyes. They were so brown that, from a distance of more than a few inches, they looked black. She smiled. "I love you."

"I love you," he said.

"I thought you were dead."

"Wasn't."

"After the lightning stopped, I called you, but you didn't answer for the longest time."

"I was busy with a call to Chicago," he said, grinning.

"Seriously."

"Okay. It was San Francisco."

"I was scared."

"I *couldn't* answer you right away," he said soothingly. "In case you've forgotten, O'Brian fell on top of me. Knocked the wind right out. He doesn't look so big, but he's as solid as a rock. I guess he builds a lot of muscles by picking lint off his suits and shining his shoes nine hours a day."

"That was a pretty brave thing you did."

"Making love to you? Think nothing of it."

Playfully, she slapped his face. "You know what I mean. You save O'Brian's life."

"Nope."

"Yes, you did. He thought so, too."

"For God's sake, I didn't step in front of him and shield him from the tree with mine own precious bod! I just pulled him out of the way. Anyone would have done the same."

She shook her head. "Wrong. Not everyone thinks as fast as you do."

"A fast thinker, huh? Yeah. That's something I'll admit to being. I'm a fast thinker, but I'm sure no hero. I won't let you pin *that* label on me because then you'll expect me to live up to it. Can you just imagine what a hell on earth Superman's life would be if he ever married Lois Lane? Her expectations would be so high!"

"Anyway," Carol said, "even if you won't admit it, O'Brian knows you saved his life, and that's the important thing."

"It is?"

"Well, I was pretty sure the adoption agency would approve us. But now there's not the slightest doubt about it."

"There's always a slim chance—"

"No," she said, interrupting him. "O'Brian's not going to fail you after you saved his life. Not a chance. He's going to wrap the recommendations committee around his finger."

Paul blinked, then slowly broke into a smile. "I'll be damned. I didn't think of that."

"So you're a hero, Papa."

"Well . . . maybe I am, Mama."

"I think I prefer 'Mom.'"

"And I prefer 'Dad.'"

"What about 'Pop'?"

"Pop isn't a name. It's a sound a champagne cork makes."

"Are you suggesting a celebration?" she asked.

"I thought we'd put on our robes, mosey down to the kitchen, and whip up an early dinner. If you're hungry, that is."

"Famished."

"You can make a mushroom salad," he said. "I'll whip up my famous fettuccine Alfredo. We've got a bottle or two of Mumm's Extra Dry we've been saving for a special occasion. We'll open that, pile our plates high with fettuccine Alfredo and mushrooms, come back up here, and have dinner in bed."

"And watch the TV news while we eat."

"Then pass the evening reading thrillers and sipping champagne until we can't keep our eyes open."

"Sounds wonderfully, sinfully lazy," she said.

More evenings than not, he spent two hours proofreading and polishing his novel. And it was an unusual night when Carol didn't have some paperwork to catch up on.

As they dressed in robes and bedroom slippers,

Paul said, "We've got to learn to take *most* evenings off. We'll have to spend plenty of time with the kid. We'll owe it to him."

"Or her."

"Or them," he said.

Her eyes shone. "You think they'll let us adopt more than one?"

"Of course they will—once we've proven we can handle the first. After all," he said self-mockingly, "am I not the hero who saved good old Al O'Brian's life?"

On their way to the kitchen, halfway down the stairs, she stopped and turned and hugged him. "We're really going to have a family."

"So it seems."

"Oh, Paul, I don't remember when I've ever been so happy. Tell me this feeling's going to last forever."

He held her, and it was very fine to have her in his arms. When you got right down to it, affection was even better than sex; being needed and loved was better than making love.

"Tell me nothing can go wrong," she said.

"Nothing can go wrong, and that feeling you have will last forever, and I'm glad you're so happy. There. How's that?"

She kissed his chin and the corners of his mouth, and he kissed her nose.

"Now," he said, "can we please get some fettuccine before I start chewing my tongue?"

"Such a romantic."

"Even romantics get hungry."

As they reached the bottom of the steps, they were startled by a sudden, loud hammering sound. It was steady but arhythmic: *Thunk, thunk, thunk-thunk-thunk, thunk-thunk*...

Carol said, "What the devil's that?"

"It's coming from outside...and above us."

They stood on the last step, looking up and back toward the second floor.

Thunk, thunk-thunk, thunk, thunk...

"Damn," Paul said. "I'll bet one of the shutters came loose in the wind." They listened for a moment, and then he sighed. "I'll have to go out and fix it."

"Now? In the rain?"

"If I don't do anything, the wind might tear it clean off the house. Worse yet, it might just hang there and clatter all night. We won't get any sleep, and neither will half the neighborhood."

She frowned. "But the lightning...Paul, after everything that's happened, I don't think you should risk climbing around on a ladder in the middle of a storm."

He didn't like the idea, either. The thought of being high on a ladder in the middle of a thunderstorm made his scalp prickle.

She said, "I don't want you to go out there if—"

The hammering stopped.

They waited.

Wind. The patter of rain. The branches of a tree scraping lightly against an outside wall.

At last, Paul said, "Too late. If it was a shutter, it's been torn off."

"I didn't hear it fall."

"It wouldn't make much noise if it dropped in the grass or the shrubbery."

"So you don't have to go out in the rain," she said,

crossing the foyer toward the short hall that led to the kitchen.

He followed her. "Yeah, but now it's a bigger repair job."

As they entered the kitchen, their footsteps echoing hollowly off the quarry-tile floor, she said, "You don't have to worry about it until tomorrow or the day after. Right now, all you've got to worry about is the sauce for the fettuccine. Don't let it curdle."

Taking a copper saucepan from a rack of gleaming utensils that hung over the center utility island, he pretended to be insulted by her remark. "Have I *ever* curdled the sauce for the fettuccine?"

"Seems to me the last time you made it, the stuff was—"

"*Never!*"

"Yes," she said teasingly. "Yes, it definitely wasn't up to par the last time." She took a plastic bag of mushrooms from the big, stainless-steel refrigerator. "Although it breaks my heart to tell you this, the last time you made fettuccine Alfredo, the sauce was as lumpy as the mattress in a ten-dollar-a-night motel."

"What a vile accusation! Besides, what makes you such an expert on ten-dollar-a-night motels? Are you leading a secret life I ought to know about?"

Together, they prepared dinner, chatting about this and that, bantering a lot, trying to amuse each other and to elicit a laugh now and then. For Paul, the world dwindled until they were the only two people in it. The universe was no larger than the warm, familiar kitchen.

Then lightning flickered, and the cozy mood was broken. It was soft lightning, nothing as dazzling and destructive as the bolts that had struck outside of

O'Brian's office a few hours ago. Nevertheless, Paul stopped talking in midsentence, his attention captured by the flash, his eyes drawn to the long, many-paned window behind the sink. On the rear lawn, the trees appeared to writhe and shimmer and ripple in the fluttering storm light, so that it seemed he was looking not at the trees themselves but at their reflections in the surface of a lake.

Suddenly, another movement caught his eye, though he wasn't sure what he was seeing. The afternoon, which had been gray and dark to begin with, was now gradually giving away to an early night, and thin fog was drifting in. Shadows lay everywhere. The meager daylight was deceptive, muddy; it distorted rather than illuminated those things it touched. In that penumbral landscape, something abruptly darted out from behind the thick trunk of an oak tree, crossed a stretch of open grass, and quickly disappeared behind a lilac bush.

Carol said, "Paul? What's wrong?"

"Someone's out on the lawn."

"In this rain? Who?"

"I don't know."

She joined him by the window. "I don't see anybody."

"Someone ran from the oak to the lilac bush. He was hunched over and moving pretty fast."

"What's he look like?"

"I can't say. I'm not even sure it was a man. Might have been a woman."

"Maybe it was just a dog."

"Too big."

"Could've been Jasper."

Jasper was the Great Dane that belonged to the

Hanrahan family, three doors down the street. He was a large, piercing-eyed, friendly animal with an amazing tolerence for small children and a liking for Oreo cookies.

"They wouldn't let Jasper out in weather like this," Paul said. "They pamper that mutt."

Lightning pulsed softly again, and a violent gust of wind whipped the trees back and forth, and rain began to fall harder than before—and in the middle of that maelstrom, something rushed out from the lilac bush.

"There!" Paul said.

The intruder crouched low, obscured by the rain and the mist, a shadow among shadows. It was illuminated so briefly and strangely by the lightning that its true appearance remained tantalizingly at the edge of perception. It loped toward the brick wall that marked the perimeter of the property, vanished for a moment in an especially dense patch of fog, reappeared as an amorphous black shape, then changed direction, paralleling the wall now, heading toward the gate at the northwest corner of the rear lawn. As the darkening sky throbbed with lightning once more, the intruder fled through electric-blue flashes, through the open gate, into the street, and away.

"Just the dog," Carol said.

Paul frowned. "I thought I saw . . ."

"What?"

"A face. A woman looking back . . . just for a second, just as she went through the gate."

"No," Carol said. "It was Jasper."

"You saw him?"

"Yes."

"Clearly?"

"Well, no, not clearly. But I could see enough to tell that it was a dog the size of a small pony, and Jasper's the only pooch around who fits that description."

"I guess Jasper's a lot smarter than he used to be."

Carol blinked. "What do you mean?"

"Well, he had to unlatch the gate to get into the yard. He never used to be able to do that trick."

"Oh, of course he didn't. We must have left the gate open."

Paul shook his head. "I'm sure it was closed when we drove up a while ago."

"Closed, maybe—but not latched. The wind pushed it open, and Jasper wandered in."

Paul stared out at the rain-slashed fog, which glowed dully with the last somber rays of the fading twilight. "I guess you're right," he said, though he was not entirely convinced. "I better go latch the gate."

"No, no," Carol said quickly. "Not while the storm's on."

"Now look here, sugarface, I'm not going to jump into bed and pull the blankets over my head every time there's a little thunder—just because of what happened this afternoon."

"I don't expect you to," she said. "But before you start dancing in the rain like Gene Kelly, you've got to let *me* get over what happened today. It's still too fresh in my mind for me to stand here watching you while you cavort across the lawn in the lightning."

"It'll only take a moment and—"

"Say, are you trying to get out of making that fettuccine?" she asked, cocking her head and looking at him suspiciously.

"Certainly not. I'll finish making it as soon as I've gone and closed the gate."

"I know what you're up to, mister," she said smugly. "You're hoping you *will* be struck by lightning because you *know* your sauce is going to turn out lumpy, and you simply can't take the humiliation."

"That's a base canard," he said, falling easily into their game again. "I make the silkiest fettuccine Alfredo this side of Rome. Silkier than Sophia Loren's thighs."

"All I know is, the last time you made it, the stuff was as lumpy as a bowl of oatmeal."

"I thought you said it was as lumpy as a mattress in a ten-dollar-a-night motel."

She lifted her head proudly. "I'm not just a one-simile woman, you know."

"How *well* I know."

"So are you going to make fettuccine—or will you take the coward's way out and get killed by lightning?"

"I'll make you eat your words," he said.

Grinning, she said, "That's easier than eating your lumpy fettuccine."

He laughed. "All right, all right. You win. I can latch the gate in the morning."

He returned to the stove, and she went back to the cutting board where she was mincing parsley and scallions for the salad dressing.

He knew she was probably right about the intruder. Most likely, it had been Jasper, chasing a cat or looking for an Oreo handout. The thing he'd thought he had seen—the slightly twisted, moon-white face of a woman, lightning reflected in her eyes, her mouth curled into a snarl of hatred or rage—had surely been a trick of light and shadow. Still, the incident left him uneasy. He could not entirely regain the warm, cozy feeling he'd had just before he'd looked out the window.

●H●H●

Grace Mitowski filled the yellow plastic bowl with Meow Mix and put it in the corner by the kitchen door.

"Kitty-kitty-kitty."

Aristophanes didn't respond.

The kitchen wasn't Ari's favorite place in the house, for it was the only room in which he was not permitted to climb wherever he wished. He wasn't actually much of a climber anyway. He lacked the spirit of adventure that many cats had, and he usually stayed on the floor. However, even though he had no burning desire to scamper up on the kitchen counters, he didn't want anyone telling him he *couldn't* do it. Like most cats, he resisted discipline and despised all rules. Nevertheless, as little as he liked the kitchen, he never failed to put in an appearance at mealtime. In fact, he was often waiting impatiently by his bowl when Grace came to fill it.

She raised her voice. "Kitty-kitty-kitty."

There was no answering meow. Aristophanes did not, as expected, come running, his tail curled up slightly, eager for his dinner.

"Ari-Ari-Ari! Soup's on, you silly cat."

She put away the box of cat food and washed her hands at the sink.

Thunk, thunk-thunk!

The hammering sound—one hard blow followed

by two equally hard blows struck close together—was so sudden and loud that Grace jerked in surprise and almost dropped the small towel on which she was drying her hands. The noise had come from the front of the house. She waited a moment, and there was only the sound of the wind and falling rain, and then—

Thunk! Thunk!

She hung the towel on the rack and stepped into the downstairs hallway.

Thunk-thunk-thunk!

She walked hesitantly down the hall to the front door and snapped on the porch light. The door had a peephole, and the fish-eye lens provided a wide view. She couldn't see anyone; the porch appeared to be deserted.

THUNK!

That blow was delivered with such force that Grace thought the door had been torn from its hinges. There was a splintering sound as she jumped back, and she expected to see chunks of wood exploding into the hall. But the door still hung firmly in place, though it vibrated noisily in its frame; the deadbolt rattled against the lock plate.

THUNK! THUNK! THUNK!

"Stop that!" she shouted. "Who are you? Who's there?"

The pounding stopped, and she thought she heard adolescent laughter.

She had been on the verge of either calling the police or going for the pistol she kept in her nightstand, but when she heard the laughter, she changed her mind. She could certainly handle a few kids without help. She wasn't so old and weak and fragile that she needed to call the cops to deal with a bunch of ornery little pranksters.

Cautiously, she drew aside the curtain on the long, narrow window beside the door. Tense, ready to step away quickly if someone made a threatening move toward the glass, she looked out. There was no one on the porch.

She heard the laughter again. It was high-pitched, musical, girlish.

Letting the curtain fall back into place, she turned to the door, unlocked it, and stepped onto the threshold.

The night wind was raw and wet. Rain drizzled off the scalloped eaves of the porch.

The immediate area in front of the house offered at least a hundred hiding places for the hoaxers. Bristling shrubbery rustled in the wind, just the other side of the railing, and the yellowish glow from the insect-repelling bulb in the porch ceiling illuminated little more than the center of the porch. The walkway that led from the bottom of the porch steps to the street was flanked by hedges that looked blue black in the darkness. Among the many shades of night, none of the pranksters were visible.

Grace waited, listened.

Thunder rumbled in the distance, but there was no laughter, no giggling in the darkness.

—*Maybe it wasn't kids.*

—*Who else?*

—*You see them on TV news all the time. The iron-eyed ones who shoot and stab and strangle people for the fun of it. They seem to be everywhere these days, the misfits, the psychopaths.*

—That was not adult laughter. This is kids' work.
—Still, maybe I better get inside and lock the door.
—Stop thinking like a frightened old lady, dammit!

It *was* odd that any of the neighborhood children would harass her, for she was on excellent terms with all of them. Of course, maybe these weren't kids from the immediate neighborhood. Just a couple of streets away, everyone was a stranger to her.

She turned and examined the outer face of the front door. She could find no indication that it had been struck repeatedly and violently only moments ago. The wood was not chipped or cracked; it wasn't even slightly marred.

She was amazed because she was certain she had heard the wood splintering. What would kids use that would make a lot of noise while leaving absolutely no marks on the door? Bean bags or something of that nature? No. A bean bag wouldn't have made such a horrendous racket; the impact of the bag against the door might have been loud, yes, very loud indeed, if it had been swung with sufficient force, but the sound wouldn't have been so hard, so sharp.

Again, she slowly scanned the yard. Nothing moved out there except the wind-stirred foliage.

For nearly a minute she watched and listened. She would have waited longer, if only to prove to any mischievous young observers that she was not a frightened old lady who could be easily intimidated; but the air was damp and chilly, and she began to worry about catching a cold.

She went inside and closed the door.

She waited with her hand on the knob, expecting the kids to return shortly. The first time they hit the door, she would jerk it open and catch them red-handed, before they could dart off the porch and hide.

Two minutes passed. Three minutes. Five.

No one hammered on the door, which was distinctly strange. To pranksters, the fun wasn't in the first assault so much as in the second and third and fourth; their intent was not to startle but to torment.

Apparently, the defiant stance she had taken in the doorway had discouraged them. Very likely, they were on their way to another house, seeking a more excitable victim.

She snapped the lock into place.

What kind of parents would allow their children to be out playing in an electrical storm like this?

Shaking her head in dismay at the irresponsibility of some parents, Grace headed back the hall, and with each step she half expected the hammering to start again. But it didn't.

She had planned to have a light, nutritious dinner of steamed vegetables covered with Cheddar cheese, accompanied by a slice or two of home-baked cornbread, but she wasn't hungry yet. She decided to watch the ABC evening news before preparing dinner—although she knew that, with the world in the state it was, the news might put her off her dinner altogether.

In the study, before she had a chance to turn on the television set and hear the latest atrocity stories, she found a mess on the seat of her big armchair. For a moment she could do nothing but stare at the ruin in disbelief: hundreds of feathers; shreds of cloth; colorful, unraveled threads that had once constituted a needlework pattern, but which now lay in a bright, meaningless tangle amidst drifts of goosedown. A couple of years ago, Carol Tracy had given her a set

of three small, exceedingly lovely, handmade needlework throw pillows. It was one of those gifts that had
been clawed to pieces and left on the armchair.

Aristophanes.

Ari hadn't ripped up anything important since he
was a kitten. An act as destructive as this was quite
out of character for him, but he was surely the culprit.
There was not really another suspect to be seriously
considered.

"Ari! Where are you hiding, you sneaky Siamese?"
She went to the kitchen.

Aristophanes was standing at the yellow bowl, eating his Meow Mix. He glanced up as she entered the
room.

"You fur-footed menace," she said. "What in the
world has gotten into you today?"

Aristophanes blinked, sneezed, rubbed his muzzle
with one paw, and returned to his dinner with lofty,
catlike indifference to her exasperation and puzzle-
ment.

●H●II●

Later that night, in her darkened bedroom, Carol
Tracy stared at the adumbral ceiling and listened to
her husband's soft, steady breathing. He had been
asleep for only a few minutes.

The night was quiet. The rain had stopped, and the
sky was no longer shaken by thunder. Occasionally,
wind brushed across the shingled roof and sighed
wearily at the windows, but the fury had gone out of
it.

Carol teetered pleasantly on the edge of sleep. She
was a bit lightheaded from the champagne she had

been slowly sipping throughout the evening, and she felt as if she were floating in warm water, with gentle waves lapping at her sides.

She thought dreamily about the child they would adopt, tried to envision its appearance. A gallery of sweet young faces filled her imagination. If it was an infant, rather than a three- or four-year-old, they would name it themselves: Jason, if a boy; Julia, if a girl. Carol rocked herself on the thin line between wakefulness and dreams by rolling those two names back and forth in her mind: *Jason, Julia, Jason, Julia, Jason . . .*

Falling off the edge, dropping into a well of sleep, she had the ugly, unwelcome thought she had resisted so strenuously earlier in the day: *Something's trying to stop us from adopting a baby.*

Then she was in a strange place where there was not much light, where something hissed and murmured sullenly just out of sight, where the purple-amber shadows had substance and crowded close with menacing intent. In that unknown place, the nightmare unrolled with the frantic, nerve-jarring rhythm of player-piano music.

At first she was running in utter lightlessness, and then she was suddenly running from one room to another in a large house, weaving through a forest of furniture, knocking over a floor lamp, banging one hip against the sharp corner of a credenza, stumbling and nearly falling over the loose edge of an oriental carpet. She plunged through an archway, into a long hall, and turned and looked back into the room from which she had come, but the room wasn't there any longer. The house existed only in front of her; behind, there was perfect, featureless blackness.

Blackness...and then a glimmer of something. A
glint. A splinter of light. A silvery, moving object.
The thing swung from side to side, vanishing into
darkness, reappearing with a gleam a second later,
vanishing again, back and forth, back and forth, rather
like a pendulum, never visible long enough to be
identified. Although she couldn't quite see what the
silvery thing was, she could tell that it was moving
toward her, and she knew she must get away from it
or die. She ran along the hall to the foot of the stairs,
climbed quickly to the second floor. She glanced back
and down, but the stairs were not there any more. Just
an inky pit. And then the brief flash of something
swinging back and forth in that pit...again...again
...like a ticking metronome. She rushed into the bedroom, slammed the door, grabbed a chair with the
intention of bracing it under the knob—and discovered that, while her back was turned, the door had
disappeared, as had the wall in which it had been set.
Where the wall had been, there was subterranean
gloom. And a silvery flicker. Very close now. Closer
still. She screamed but made no sound, and the mys-
teriously gleaming object arced over her head and—

(Thunk!)

—This is more than just a dream, she thought desperately. Much more than that. This is a memory, a
prophecy, a warning. This is a—

(Thunk!)

—She was running in another house that was altogether different from the first. This place was
smaller, the furnishings less grand. She did not know
where she was, yet she knew she had been here before.
The house was familiar, just as the first place had
been. She hurried through a doorway, into a kitchen.

Two bloody, severed heads were on the kitchen table. One of them was a man's head, and the other was a woman's. She recognized them, felt that she knew them well, but was unable to think of their names. The four dead eyes were wide but sightless; the two mouths gaped, the swollen tongues protruding over the purple lips. As Carol stood transfixed by that grisly sight, the dead eyes rolled in their sockets and focused on her. The cold lips twisted into icy smiles. Carol turned, intending to flee, but there was only a void behind her and a glint of light off the hard surface of something silvery and then—

(Thunk!)

—She was running through a mountain meadow in reddish, late-afternoon light. The grass was knee-high, and the trees loomed ahead of her. When she looked over her shoulder, the meadow was no longer back there. Only blackness, as before. And the rhythmically swinging, shimmering, steadily approaching *thing* to which she was unable to fix a name. Gasping, her heart racing, she ran faster, reached the trees, glanced back once more, saw that she had not run nearly fast enough to escape, cried out and—

(Thunk!)

For a long time the nightmare shifted from one of those three dreamscapes to the other—from the first house to the meadow to the second house to the meadow to the first house again—until at last she woke with an unvoiced scream caught in her throat. She sat straight up, shuddering. She was cold and yet slick with sweat; she slept in just a T-shirt and panties, and both garments clung to her skin, unpleasantly sticky. The frightening sound from the nightmare continued to echo in her mind—*thunk, thunk, thunk-*

thunk, thunk—and she realized that her subconscious had borrowed that noise from reality, from the wind-loosened shutter that had startled her and Paul earlier. Gradually, the pounding noise faded and blended with the thumping of her heart.

She drew back the covers and swung her bare legs out of bed. She sat on the edge of the mattress, hugging herself.

Dawn had come. Gray light seeped in around the drapes; it was too dim to reveal the details of the furniture, but it was just bright enough to deepen the shadows and distort the shapes of everything, so that the room seemed like an alien place.

The rain had stopped a couple of hours before she'd gone to bed, but the storm had returned while she'd been sleeping. Rain pattered on the roof and gurgled through the gutters and the downspouts. Low thunder rumbled like a distant cannonade.

Paul was still asleep, snoring softly.

Carol knew she wouldn't be able to get back to sleep. Like it or not, rested or not, she was up for the day.

Without turning on a light, she went into the master bathroom. In the weak glow of dawn, she stripped out of her damp T-shirt and panties. While soaping herself in the shower, she thought about the nightmare, which had been considerably more vivid than any dream she'd ever had before.

That strange, jarring sound—*thunk, thunk*—had been the most frightening thing in the dream, and the memory of it still nagged her. It wasn't just an ordinary hammering noise; there was an odd echo to it, a hardness and sharpness she couldn't quite define. She decided it was not *only* a case of her subconscious mind borrowing the noise the shutter had made earlier. The terrifying sound in the dream was caused by something considerably more disturbing than the mere banging of an unmoored shutter. Furthermore, she was sure she had heard *precisely* that sound on another occasion, too. Not in the nightmare. In real life. In another place . . . a long time ago . . .

As she let the hot water stream over her, sluicing away the soap, she tried to recall where and when she had heard exactly that same unsettling sound, for it suddenly seemed important for her to identify it. Without understanding why, she felt vaguely threatened as long as she could not recall the source of the sound. But remembrance hung tantalizingly beyond the limits of her reach, like the title of a hauntingly familiar but unnameable piece of music.

4

At 8:45, after breakfast, Carol left for work, and Paul went upstairs to the rear bedroom that he had converted into an office. He had created a Spartan atmosphere in which to write without distraction. The off-white walls were bare, unadorned by even a single painting. The room contained only an inexpensive desk, a typist's chair, an electric typewriter, a jar bristling with pens and pencils, a deep letter tray that now contained nearly two hundred manuscript pages of the novel he had started at the beginning of his sabbatical, a telephone, a three-shelf bookcase filled with reference works, a bottled-water dispenser in one corner, and a small table upon which stood a Mr. Coffee machine.

This morning, as usual, he prepared a pot of coffee first thing. Just as he pressed the switch labeled BREWER and poured water into the top of the Mr.

Coffee, the telephone rang. He sat on the edge of the desk, picked up the receiver. "Hello."

"Paul? Grace Mitowski."

"Good morning, love. How are you?"

"Well, these old bones don't like rainy weather, but otherwise I'm coping."

Paul smiled. "Listen, I know you can still run circles around me any time."

"Nonsense. You're a compulsive worker with a guilt complex about leisure. Not even a nuclear reactor has your energy."

He laughed. "Don't psychoanalyze me, Grace. I get enough of that from my wife."

"Speaking of whom..."

"Sorry, but you just missed her. You ought to be able to catch her at the office in half an hour."

Grace hesitated.

Hot coffee began to drizzle into the Pyrex pot, and the aroma of it swiftly filled the room.

Sensing tension in Grace's hesitation, Paul said, "What's wrong?"

"Well..." She cleared her throat nervously. "Paul, how *is* she? She's not ill or anything?"

"Carol? Oh, no. Of course not."

"You're sure? I mean, you know that girl's like a daughter to me. If anything was wrong, I'd want to know."

"She's fine. Really. In fact she had a physical exam last week. The adoption agency required it. Both of us passed with flying colors."

Grace was silent again.

Frowning, Paul said, "Why are you worried all of a sudden?"

"Well... you'll think old Gracie is losing her marbles, but I've had two disturbing dreams, one during a nap yesterday, the other last night, and Carol was in both. I seldom dream, so when I have *two* nightmares and wake up both times feeling I've got to warn Carol . . ."

"Warn her about what?"

"I don't know. All I remember about the dreams is that Carol was in them. I woke up thinking: *It's coming. I've got to warn Carol that it's coming.* I know that sounds silly. And don't ask me what 'it' might be. I can't remember. But I feel Carol's in danger. Now Lord knows, I don't believe in dream prophecies and garbage like that. I *think* I don't believe in them—yet here I am calling you about this."

The coffee was ready. Paul leaned over, turned off the brewer. "The strange thing is—Carol and I were nearly hurt in a freak accident yesterday." He told her about the damage at O'Brian's office.

"Good God," she said, "I saw that lightning when I woke up from my nap, but it never occurred to me that you and Carol . . . that the lightning might be the very thing I was . . . the very thing my *dream* oh, hell! I'm afraid to say it because I might sound like a superstitious old fool, but here goes anyway: *Was* there actually something prophetic about that dream? Did I foresee the lightning strike a few minutes before it happened?"

"If nothing else," Paul said uneasily, "it's at least a remarkable coincidence."

They were silent for a moment, wondering, and then she said, "Listen, Paul, I don't recall that we've ever discussed this subject much before, but tell me—do *you* believe in dream prophecies, clairvoyance, things of that nature?"

"I don't believe, and I don't disbelieve. I've never really made up my mind."

"I've always been so smug about it. Always considered it a pack of lies, delusions, or just plain nonsense. But after this—"

"You're reconsidering."

"Let's just say a tiny doubt has cropped up. And now I'm more worried about Carol than I was when I called you."

"Why? I told you she wasn't even scratched."

"She escaped once," Grace said, "but I had *two* dreams, and one of them came to me hours after the lightning. So maybe the 'it' is something else. I mean, if the first dream had some truth in it, then maybe the second does, too. God, isn't this crazy? If you start believing in just a little bit of this nonsense, you get carried away with it real fast. But I can't help it. I'm still concerned about her."

"Even if your first dream was prophetic," Paul said, "the second one was probably just a repeat of it, an echo, not a whole new dream."

"You think so?"

"Sure. This never happened to you before, so why should it happen again? Most likely, it was just a freak thing . . . like the lightning yesterday."

"Yeah, I guess you're probably right," she said, sounding somewhat relieved. "Maybe it could happen once. Maybe I can accept that. But I'm not Edgar Cayce or Nostradamus. And I can guarantee you I'm never going to be writing a weekly column of predictions for the *National Enquirer*."

Paul laughed.

"Still," she said, "I wish I could remember exactly

what happened in *both* those nightmares."

They talked a while longer, and when Paul finally hung up, he stared at the receiver for a moment, frowning. Although he was pretty much convinced that the timing of Grace's dream had been merely a strange coincidence, he was nonetheless affected by it, more profoundly affected than seemed reasonable.

It's coming.

The moment Grace had voiced those two words, Paul had felt a gut-deep, bone-deep chill.

It's coming.

Coincidence, he told himself. Sheer coincidence and nonsense. Forget about it.

Gradually he became aware, once again, of the rich aroma of hot coffee. He rose from the edge of the desk and filled a mug with the steaming brew.

For a minute or two he stood at the window behind the desk, sipping coffee, staring out at the dirty, scudding clouds and at the incessant rain. Eventually he lowered his gaze and looked down into the rear yard, instantly recalling the intruder he had seen last evening while he and Carol had been making dinner: that briefly glimpsed, pale, distorted, lightning-illuminated face; a woman's face; shining eyes; mouth twisted into a snarl of rage or hatred. Or perhaps it had just been Jasper, the Great Dane, and a trick of light.

THUNK!

The sound was so loud and unexpected that Paul jumped in surprise. If his mug hadn't been half empty, he would have spilled coffee all over the carpet.

THUNK! THUNK!

It couldn't be the same shutter they'd heard last

evening, for it would have continued banging all night. Which meant there were now two of them to repair.

Jeez, he thought, the old homestead is falling down around my ears.

THUNK!

The source of the sound was nearby; in fact it was so close that it seemed to originate within the room.

Paul pressed his forehead against the cool window glass, peered out to the left, then to the right, trying to see if that pair of shutters was in place. As far as he could see, they were both properly anchored.

Thunk, thunk-thunk, thunk, thunk . . .

The noise grew softer but settled into a steady, arhythmical beat that was more irritating than the louder blows had been. And now it seemed to be coming from another part of the house.

Although he didn't want to get up on a ladder and fix a shutter in the rain, that was exactly what had to be done, for he couldn't get any writing accomplished with that constant clattering to distract him. At least there hadn't been any lightning this morning.

He put his mug on the desk and started out of the room. Before he reached the door, the telephone rang.

So it's going to be one of *those* days, he thought wearily.

Then he realized that the shutter had stopped banging the moment the phone had rung. Maybe the wind had wrenched it loose of the house, in which case repairs could wait until the weather improved.

He returned to his desk and answered the telephone. It was Alfred O'Brian, from the adoption agency. Initially, the conversation was awkward, and Paul was embarrassed by it. O'Brian insisted on expressing his gratitude: "You saved my life; you really did!" He was equally insistent about repeatedly and quite unnecessarily apologizing for his failure to express that gratitude yesterday, immediately following the incident in his office: "But I was so shaken, stunned, I just wasn't thinking clearly enough to thank you, which was unforgivable of me." Each time Paul protested at the mention of words like "heroic," and "brave," O'Brian became even more vociferous than before. At last, Paul stifled his objections and allowed the man to get it out of his system; O'Brian was determined to cleanse his conscience in much the same way that he fussed with the minute specks of lint on his suit jacket. Finally, however, he seemed to feel he had atoned for his (largely imaginary) thoughtlessness, and Paul was relieved when the conversation changed directions.

O'Brian had a second reason for calling, and he got straight to it now, as if he, too, was suddenly embarrassed. He could not (he explained with more apologies) locate the application form that the Tracys had brought to his office the previous day. "Of course, when that tree crashed through the window, it scattered a lot of papers all over the floor. A terrible mess. Some of them were rumpled and dirty when we gathered them up, and a great many of them were damp from the rain. In spite of that, Margie, my secretary, was able to put them in order—except, of course, for your application. We can't find it anywhere. I suppose it might have blown out through one of the broken windows. I don't know why your papers should be the only ones we've lost, and of course we must have a completed, signed application before we can present your names to the recommendations committee. I'm extremely sorry about this inconvenience, Mr. Tracy, I truly am."

"It wasn't your fault," Paul said. "I'll just stop in later today and pick up another form. Carol and I can fill it out and sign it tonight."

"Good," O'Brian said. "I'm glad to hear that. It has to be back in my hands early tomorrow morning if we're going to make the next meeting of the committee. Margie needs three full business days to run the required verifications on the information in your application, and that's just about how much time we have before next Wednesday's committee meeting. If we miss that session, there's not another one for two weeks."

"I'll be in to pick up the form before noon," Paul assured him. "And I'll have it back to you first thing Friday morning."

They exchanged goodbyes, and Paul put down the phone.

THUNK!

When he heard that sound, he sagged, dispirited. He was going to have to fix a shutter after all. And then drive into the city to pick up the new application. And then drive home. And by the time he did all of that, half the day would be shot, and he wouldn't have written a single word.

THUNK! THUNK!

"Dammit," he said.

Thunk, thunk-thunk, thunk-thunk . . .

It definitely was going to be one of *those* days.

He went downstairs to the hall closet where he kept his raincoat and galoshes.

●H●H●

The windshield wipers flogged back and forth, back and forth, with a short, shrill squeak that made Carol grit her teeth. She hunched forward a bit, over the steering wheel, squinting through the streaming rain.

The streets glistened; the macadam was slick, greasy looking. Dirty water raced along the gutters and formed filthy pools around clogged drainage grids.

At ten minutes past nine, the morning rush hour was just over. Although the streets were still moderately busy, traffic was moving smoothly and swiftly. In fact everyone was driving too fast to suit Carol, and she hung back a little, watchful and cautious.

Two blocks from her office, her caution proved justified, but it still wasn't enough to avert disaster altogether. Without bothering to look for oncoming traffic, a young blond woman stepped out from between two vans, directly into the path of the VW Rabbit.

"Christ!" Carol said, ramming her foot down on the brake pedal so hard that she lifted herself up off the seat.

The blonde glanced up and froze, wide-eyed.

Although the VW was moving at only twenty miles an hour, there was no hope of stopping it in time. The brakes shrieked. The tires bit—but also skidded—on the wet pavement.

God, no! Carol thought with a sick, sinking feeling.

The car hit the blonde and lifted her off the ground, tossed her backwards onto the hood, and then the rear end of the VW began to slide around to the left, into the path of an oncoming Cadillac, and the Caddy swerved, brakes squealing, and the other driver hit his horn as if he thought a sufficient volume of sound might magically push Carol safely out of his way, and for an instant she was certain they would collide, but the Caddy slid past without scraping, missing her by only an inch or two—all of this in two or three or four seconds—and at the same time the blonde rolled off the hood, toward the right side, the curb side, and the VW came to a full stop, sitting aslant the street, rocking on its springs as if it were a child's hobby horse.

●||●||●

None of the shutters was missing. Not one. None of them was loose and flapping in the wind, as Paul had thought.

Wearing galoshes and a raincoat with a hood, he walked all the way around the house, studying each set of shutters on the first and second floors, but he couldn't see anything amiss. The place showed no sign of storm damage.

Perplexed, he circled the house again, each step resulting in a squishing noise as the rain-saturated lawn gave like a sodden sponge beneath him. This time around, he looked for broken tree limbs that might be swinging against the walls when the wind gusted. The trees were all intact.

Shivering in the unseasonably chilly autumn air, he just stood on the lawn for a minute or two, cocking his head to the right and then to the left, listening for the pounding that had filled the house moments ago. He couldn't hear it now. The only sounds were the soughing wind, the rustling trees, and the rain driving into the grass with a soft, steady hiss.

At last, his face numbed by the cold wind and by

the heat-leaching rain, he decided to halt his search until the pounding started again and gave him something to get a fix on. Meanwhile, he could drive downtown and pick up the application form at the adoption agency. He put one hand to his face, felt his beard stubble, remembered Alfred O'Brian's compulsive neatness, and figured he ought to shave before he went.

He reentered the house by way of the screened-in rear porch, leaving his dripping coat on a vinyl-upholstered glider and shedding his galoshes before going into the kitchen. Inside, he closed the door behind him and basked for a moment in the warm air.

THUNK! THUNK! THUNK!

The house shuddered as if it had received three extremely hard, rapid blows from the enormous fist of a giant. Above the kitchen's central utility island, where a utensil rack was suspended from the ceiling, copper pots and pans swung on their hooks and clattered against one another.

THUNK!

The wall clock rattled on its hook; if it had been any less firmly attached than it was, it would have flung itself off the wall, onto the floor.

Paul moved toward the middle of the room, trying to ascertain the direction from which the pounding was coming.

THUNK! THUNK!

The oven door fell open.

The two dozen small jars nestled in the spice rack began to clink against one another.

What the hell is happening here? he wondered uneasily.

THUNK!

He turned slowly, listening, seeking.

The pots and pans clattered again, and a large ladle slipped from its hook and fell with a clang to the butcher-block work surface that lay under it.

Paul looked up at the ceiling, tracking the sound.

THUNK!

He expected to see the plaster crack, but it didn't. Nevertheless, the source of the sound was definitely overhead.

Thunk, thunk-thunk, thunk . . .

The pounding suddenly grew quieter than it had been, but it didn't fade away altogether. At least the house stopped quivering, and the cooking utensils stopped banging together.

Paul headed for the stairs, determined to track down the cause of the disturbance.

●‖●‖●

The blonde was in the gutter, flat on her back, one arm out at her side with the palm up and the hand slack, the other arm draped across her belly. Her golden hair was muddy. A three-inch-deep stream of water surged around her, carrying leaves and grit and scraps of paper litter toward the nearest storm drain, and her long hair fanned out around her head and rippled silkily in those filthy currents.

Carol knelt beside the woman and was shocked to see that the victim wasn't actually a woman at all. She was a girl, no older than fourteen or fifteen. She was exceptionally pretty, with delicate features, and at the moment she was frighteningly pale.

She was also inadequately dressed for inclement weather. She wore white tennis shoes, jeans, and a blue and white checkered blouse. She had neither a raincoat nor an umbrella.

With trembling hands, Carol lifted the girl's right arm and felt the wrist for a pulse. She found the beat at once; it was strong and steady.

"Thank God," Carol said shakily. "Thank God, thank God."

She began to examine the girl for bleeding. There did not seem to be any serious injuries, no major blood loss, just a few shallow cuts and abrasions. Unless, of course, the bleeding was internal.

The driver of the Cadillac, a tall man with a goatee, stepped around the end of the VW Rabbit and looked down at the injured girl. "Is she dead?"

"No," Carol said. She gently thumbed back one of the girl's eyelids, then the other. "Just unconscious. Probably a mild concussion. Is anyone calling an ambulance?"

"I don't know," he said.

"Then you call one. Quickly."

He hurried away, splashing through a puddle that was deeper than the tops of his shoes.

Carol pressed down on the girl's chin; the jaw was slack, and the mouth fell open easily. There was no visible obstruction, no blood, nothing that might choke her, and her tongue was in a safe position.

A gray-haired woman in a transparent plastic raincoat, carrying a red and orange umbrella, appeared out of the rain. "It wasn't your fault," she told Carol. "I saw it happen. I saw it all. The child darted out in front of you without looking. There wasn't a thing you could have done to prevent it."

"I saw it, too," said a portly man who didn't quite fit under his black umbrella. "I saw the kid walking down the street like she was in a trance or something. No coat, no umbrella. Eyes kind of blank. She stepped off the curb, between those two vans, and just stood there for a few seconds, like she was just waiting for someone to come along so she could step out and get herself killed. And by God, that's what happened."

"She's not dead," Carol said, unable to keep a tremor out of her voice. "There's a first-aid kit on the back seat of my car. Will one of you get it for me?"

"Sure," the portly man said, turning toward the VW.

The first-aid kit contained, among other things, a packet of tongue depressors, and Carol wanted to have those handy. Although the unconscious girl didn't appear to be headed for imminent convulsions, Carol intended to be prepared for the worst.

A crowd had begun to gather.

A siren sounded a couple of blocks away, approaching fast. It was probably the police; the ambulance couldn't have made it so fast.

"Such a pretty child," the gray-haired woman said, staring down at the stricken girl.

Other onlookers murmured in agreement.

Carol stood up and stripped out of her raincoat. There was no point in covering the girl, for she was already as wet as she could get. Instead, Carol folded the coat, knelt down again, and carefully slipped the makeshift pillow under the victim, elevating her head just a bit above the gushing water.

The girl didn't open her eyes or stir in any way whatsoever. A tangled strand of golden hair had fallen across her face, and Carol carefully pushed it aside for her. The girl's skin was hot to the touch, fevered, in spite of the cold rain that bathed it.

Suddenly, while her fingers were still touching the girl's cheek, Carol felt dizzy and was unable to get her breath. For a moment she thought she was going to pass out and collapse on top of the unconscious teenager. A black wave rose behind her eyes, and then in that darkness there was a brief flash of silver, a glint of light off a moving object, the mysterious thing from her nightmare.

She gritted her teeth, shook her head, and refused to be swept away in that dark wave. She pulled her hand away from the girl's cheek, put it to her own face; the dizzy spell passed as abruptly as it had come. Until the ambulance arrived, she was responsible for the injured girl, and she was determined not to fail in that responsibility.

Huffing slightly, the portly man hurried back with the first-aid kit. Carol took one of the tongue depressors out of its crisp cellophane wrapper—just in case.

A police car rounded the corner and stopped behind the Volkswagen. Its revolving emergency beacons splashed red light across the wet pavement and appeared to transform the puddles of rainwater into pools of blood.

As the squad car's siren died with a growl, another, more distant siren became audible. To Carol, that warbling, high-pitched wail was the sweetest sound in the world.

The horror is almost over, she thought.

But then she looked at the girl's chalk-white face, and her relief was clouded with doubt. Perhaps the horror wasn't over after all; perhaps it had only just begun.

●11●11●

Upstairs, Paul walked slowly from room to room, listening to the hammering sound.

Thunk . . . thunk . . .

The source was still overhead. In the attic. Or on the roof.

The attic stairs were behind a paneled door at the end of the second-floor hallway. They were narrow, unpainted, and they creaked as Paul climbed them.

Although the attic had full flooring, it was not otherwise a finished room. The construction of the walls was open for inspection; the pink fiber glass insulation, which somewhat resembled raw meat, and the regularly spaced supporting studs, like ribs of bone, were visible. Two naked, hundred-watt bulbs furnished light, and shadows coiled everywhere, especially toward the eaves. For all of its length and for half of its width, the attic was high enough to allow Paul to walk through it without stooping.

The patter of rain on the roof was more than just a patter up here. It was a steady hissing, a soft, all-encompassing roar.

Nevertheless, the other sound was audible above the drumming of the rain: *Thunk . . . thunk-thunk . . .*

Paul moved slowly past stacks of cardboard cartons and other items that had been consigned to storage: a pair of large touring trunks; an old six-pronged coat rack; a tarnished brass floor lamp; two busted-out, cane-bottomed chairs that he intended to restore some day. A thin film of whitish dust draped shroudlike over all the contents of the room.

Thunk . . . thunk . . .

He walked the length of the attic, then slowly returned to the center of it and stopped. The source of the sound seemed to be directly in front of his face, only inches away. But there was nothing here that could possibly be the cause of the disturbance; nothing moved.

Thunk . . . thunk . . . thunk . . . thunk . . .

Although the hammering was softer now than it had been a few minutes ago, it was still solid and forceful; it reverberated through the frame of the house. The pounding had acquired a monotonously simple rhythm, too; each blow was separated from the ones before and after it by equal measures of time, resulting in a pattern not unlike the beating of a heart.

Paul stood in the attic, in the dust, smelling the musty odor common to all unused places, trying to get a fix on the sound, trying to understand how it could be coming out of thin air, and gradually his attitude toward the disturbance changed. He had been thinking of it as nothing more than the audible evidence of storm damage to the house, as nothing more than tedious and perhaps expensive repairs that might have to be made, an interruption in his writing schedule, an inconvenience, nothing more. But as he turned his head from side to side and squinted into every shadow, as he listened to the relentless thudding, he suddenly perceived that there was something ominous about the sound.

Thunk . . . thunk . . . thunk . . .

For reasons he could not define, the noise now seemed threatening, malevolent.

He felt colder in this sheltered place than he had felt outside in the wind and rain.

●‖●‖●

Carol wanted to ride to the hospital in the ambulance with the injured girl, but she knew she would only be in the way. Besides, the first police officer on the scene, a curly-headed young man named Tom Weatherby, needed to get a statement from her.

They sat in the front seat of the patrol car, which smelled like the peppermint lozenges on which Weatherby was sucking. The windows were made opaque by shimmering streams of rain. The police radio sputtered and crackled.

Weatherby frowned. "You're soaked to the skin. I've got a blanket in the trunk. I'll get it for you."

"No, no," she said. "I'll be fine." Her green knit suit had become saturated. Her rain-drenched hair was pasted to her head and hung slackly to her shoulders. At the moment, however, she didn't care about her appearance or about the goosebumps that prickled her skin. "Let's just get this over with."

"Well . . . if you're sure you're okay."

"I'm sure."

As he turned up the thermostat on the car heater, Weatherby said, "By any chance, do you know the kid who stepped in front of your car?"

"Know her? No. Of course not."

"She didn't have any ID on her. Did you notice if she was carrying a purse when she walked into the street?"

"I can't say for sure."

"Try to remember."

"I don't think she was."

"Probably not," he said. "After all, if she goes walking in a storm like this without a raincoat or an umbrella, why would she bother to take a purse? We'll search the street anyway. Maybe she dropped it somewhere."

"What happens if you can't find out who she is? How will you get in touch with her parents? I mean, she shouldn't be alone at a time like this."

"No problem," Weatherby said. "She'll tell us her name when she regains consciousness."

"*If* she does."

"Hey, she will. There's no need to be concerned about that. She didn't seem seriously injured."

Carol worried about it nonetheless.

For the next ten minutes, Weatherby asked questions, and she answered them. When he finished filling out the accident report, she quickly read over it, then signed at the bottom.

"You're in the clear," Weatherby said. "You were driving under the speed limit, and three witnesses say the girl stepped out of a blind spot right in front of you, without bothering to look for traffic. It wasn't your fault."

"I should have been more careful."

"I don't see what else you could have done."

"Something. Surely I could have done something," she said miserably.

He shook his head. "No. Listen, Dr. Tracy, I've seen this sort of thing happen before. There's an accident, and somebody's hurt, and nobody's really to blame—yet one of the people involved has a misplaced sense of responsibility and insists on feeling guilty. And in this case, if there *is* anybody to blame, it's the kid herself, not you. According to the witnesses, she was behaving strangely just before you turned the corner, almost as if she *intended* to get herself run down."

"But why would such a pretty girl want to throw herself in front of a car?"

Weatherby shrugged. "You told me you were a psychiatrist. You specialize in children and teenagers, right?"

"Yes."

"So you must know all the answers better than I do. Why would she want to kill herself? Could be trouble at home—a father who drinks too much and makes heavy passes at his own little girl, a mother who doesn't want to hear about it. Or maybe the kid was just jilted by her boyfriend and thinks the world is coming to an end. Or just discovered she was pregnant and decided she couldn't face her folks with the news. There must be hundreds of reasons, and I'm sure you've heard most of them in your line of work."

What he said was true, but it didn't make Carol feel better.

If only I'd been driving slower, she thought. If only I'd been quicker to react, maybe that poor girl wouldn't be in the hospital now.

"She might have been on drugs, too," Weatherby said. "Too damned many kids fool around with dope these days. I swear, some of them'll swallow any pill they're given. If it isn't something that can be swallowed, they'll sniff it or stick it in a vein. This kid you hit might have been so high she didn't even know where she was when she stepped in front of your car. Now, if that's the case, are you going to tell me it's *still* somehow your fault?"

Carol leaned back in the seat, closed her eyes, and let her breath out with a shudder. "God, I don't know *what* to tell you. All I know is . . . I feel wrung out."

"That's perfectly natural, after what you've just been through. But it isn't natural to feel guilty about this. It wasn't your fault, so don't dwell on it. Put it behind you and get on with your life."

She opened her eyes, looked at him, and smiled. "You know, Officer Weatherby, I have a hunch you'd make a pretty good psychotherapist."

He grinned. "Or a terrific bartender."

Carol laughed.

"Feeling better?" he asked.

"A little bit."

"Promise me you won't lose any sleep over this."

"I'll try not to," she said. "But I'm still concerned about the girl. Do you know which hospital they've taken her to?"

"I can find out," he said.

"Would you do that for me? I'd like to go talk to the doctor who's handling her case. If he tells me she's going to be all right, I'll find it a whole lot easier to take your advice about getting on with my life."

Weatherby picked up the microphone and asked the police dispatcher to find out where the injured girl had been taken.

●||●||●

The television antenna!

Standing in the attic, staring up at the roof above his head, Paul laughed out loud when he realized what was causing the pounding noise. The sound wasn't coming out of the empty air in front of his face, which was what he had thought for one unsettling moment. It was coming from the roof, where the television antenna was anchored. They had subscribed to cable TV a year ago, but they hadn't removed the old antenna. It was a large, directional, remote-control model affixed to a heavy brace-plate; the plate was bolted through the shingles and attached directly to a roof beam. Apparently, a nut or some other fastener had loosened slightly, and the wind was tugging at the antenna, rocking the brace-plate up and down on one of its bolts, slamming it repeatedly against the roof. The solution to the big mystery was amusingly mundane.

Or was it?

Thunk . . . thunk . . . thunk . . .

The sound was softer now than ever before, barely audible above the roar of the rain on the roof, and it was easy to believe that the antenna could be the cause of it. Gradually, however, as Paul considered this answer to the puzzle, he began to doubt if it was the *correct* answer. He thought about how loud and violent the pounding had been a few minutes ago when he had been in the kitchen: the entire house quivering, the oven door falling open, bottles rattling in the spice rack. Could a loose antenna really generate so much noise and vibration?

Thunk . . . thunk . . .

As he stared up at the ceiling, he tried to make himself believe unequivocally in the antenna theory. If it was striking a roof beam in precisely the right way, at a very special angle, so that the impact was transmitted through the entire frame of the house, perhaps a loose antenna *could* cause the pots and pans to clatter against one another in the kitchen and could make it seem as if the ceilings were about to crack. After all, if you set up exactly the right vibrations in a steel suspension bridge, you could bring it to ruin in less than a minute, regardless of the number of bolts and welds and cables holding it together. And although Paul didn't believe there was even a remote danger of a loose antenna causing that kind of apocalyptic destruction to a wood-frame house, he knew that moderate force, applied with calculation and pin-point accuracy, could have an effect quite out of proportion to the amount of energy expended. Besides, the TV antenna *had* to be the root of the disturbance, for it was the only explanation he had left.

The hammering noise became even softer and then faded altogether. He waited for a minute or two, but the only sound was the rain on the shingles overhead.

The wind must have changed direction. In time it would change back again, and the antenna would begin to rock on its brace-plate, and the pounding would start once more.

As soon as the storm was over, he would have to get the extension ladder out of the garage, go up onto the roof, and dismantle the antenna. He should have taken care of that chore shortly after they had subscribed to the cable television service. Now, because he had delayed, he was going to lose precious writing time—and at one of the most difficult and crucial points in his manuscript. That prospect frustrated him and made him nervous.

He decided to shave, drive downtown, and pick up the new set of application papers at the adoption agency. The storm might pass by the time he got home again. If it did, if he could be on the roof by eleven-thirty, he ought to be able to tear down the antenna, then have a bite of lunch, and work on his book all afternoon, barring further interruptions. But he suspected there *would* be further interruptions. He had already resigned himself to the fact that it was one of those days.

As he left the attic and turned out the lights, the house quivered under another blow.

THUNK!

Just one this time.

Then all was quiet again.

●‖●‖●

The visitors' lounge at the hospital looked like an explosion in a clown's wardrobe. The walls were canary yellow; the chairs were bright red; the carpet was orange; the magazine racks and end tables were made of heavy purple plastic; and the two large abstract paintings were done primarily in shades of blue and green.

The lounge—obviously the work of a designer who had read too much about the various psychological mood theories of color—was supposed to be positive, life-affirming. It was supposed to lift the spirits of visitors and take their minds off sick friends and dying relatives. In Carol, however, the determinedly cheery decor elicited the opposite reaction from that which the designer had intended. It was a frenetic room; it abraded the nerves as effectively as coarse sandpaper would abrade a stick of butter.

She sat on one of the red chairs, waiting for the doctor who had treated the injured girl. When he came, his stark white lab coat contrasted so boldly with the flashy decor that he appeared to radiate a saintlike aura.

Carol rose to meet him, and he asked if she was Mrs. Tracy, and he said his name was Sam Hannaport. He was tall, very husky, square-faced, florid, in his early fifties. He looked as if he would be loud and gruff, perhaps even obnoxious, but in fact he was soft-spoken and seemed genuinely concerned about how the accident had affected Carol both physically and emotionally. It took her a couple of minutes to assure him that she was all right on both counts, and then they sat down on facing red chairs.

Hannaport raised his bushy eyebrows and said, "You look as if you could use a hot bath and a big glassful of warm brandy."

"I was soaked to the skin," she said, "but I'm pretty well dried out now. What about the girl?"

"Cuts, contusions, abrasions," he said.

"Internal bleeding?"

"Nothing showed up on the tests."

"Fractures?"

"Not a broken bone in her body. She came through it amazingly well. You couldn't have been driving very fast when you hit her."

"I wasn't. But considering the way she slipped up onto the hood and then rolled off into the gutter, I thought maybe . . ." Carol shuddered, unwilling to put words to what she had thought.

"Well, the kid's in good condition now. She regained consciousness in the ambulance, and she was alert by the time I saw her."

"Thank God."

"There's no indication that she's even mildly concussed. I don't foresee any lasting effects."

Relieved, Carol sagged back in the red chair. "I'd like to see her, talk to her."

"She's resting now," Dr. Hannaport said. "I don't want her disturbed at the moment. But if you'd like to come back this evening, during visiting hours, she'll be able to see you then."

"I'll do that. I'll definitely do that." She blinked. "Good heavens, I haven't even asked you what her name is."

His bushy eyebrows rose again. "Well, we've got a small problem about that."

"Problem?" Carol tensed up again. "What do you mean? Can't she remember her name?"

"She hasn't remembered it yet, but—"

"Oh, God."

"—she will."

"You said no concussion—"

"I swear to you, it *isn't* serious," Hannaport said. He took her left hand in his big hard hands and held it as if it might crack and crumble at any moment. "Please don't excite yourself about this. The girl is going to be fine. Her inability to remember her name isn't a symptom of severe concussion or any serious brain injury; not in her case, anyway. She isn't confused or disoriented. Her field of vision is normal, and she has excellent depth perception. We tested her thought processes with some math problems—addition, subtraction, multiplication—and she got them all correct. She can spell any word you throw at her; she's a damn good speller, that one. So she's not severely concussed. She's simply suffering from mild amnesia. It's selective amnesia, you understand, just a loss of personal memories, not a loss of skills and education and whole blocks of social concepts. She hasn't forgotten how to read and write, thank God; she's only forgotten who she is, where she came from, and how she got to this place. Which sounds more serious than it really is. Of course, she's disconcerted and apprehensive. But selective amnesia is the easiest kind to recover from."

"I know," Carol said. "But somehow that doesn't make me feel a whole hell of a lot better."

Hannaport squeezed her hand firmly and gently.

"This kind of amnesia is only very, very rarely permanent or even long-lasting. She'll most likely remember who she is before dinnertime."

"If she doesn't?"

"Then the police will find out who she is, and the minute she hears her name, the mists will clear."

"She wasn't carrying any ID."

"I know," he said. "I've talked to the police."

"So what happens if they can't find out who she is?"

"They will." He patted her hand one last time, then let go.

"I don't see how you can be so sure."

"Her parents will file a missing-persons report. They'll have a photograph of her. When the police see the photograph, they'll make a connection. It'll be as simple as that."

She frowned. "What if her parents *don't* report her missing?"

"Why wouldn't they?"

"Well, what if she's a runaway from out of state? Even if her folks did file a missing-persons report back in her hometown, the police here wouldn't necessarily be aware of it."

"The last time I looked, runaway kids favored New York City, California, Florida—just about any place besides Harrisburg, Pennsylvania."

"There's always an exception to any rule."

Hannaport laughed softly and shook his head. "If pessimism were a competitive sport, you'd win the world series."

She blinked in surprise, then smiled. "I'm sorry. I guess I am being excessively gloomy."

Glancing at his watch, getting up from his chair,

he said, "Yes, I think you are. Especially considering how well the girl came through it all. It could have been a lot worse."

Carol got to her feet, too. In a rush, the words falling over one another, she said, "I guess maybe the reason it bothers me so much is because I deal with disturbed children every day, and it's my job to help them get well again, and that's all I ever wanted to do since I was in high school—work with sick kids, be a healer—but now I'm responsible for all the pain this poor girl is going through."

"You mustn't feel that way. You didn't *intend* to harm her."

Carol nodded. "I know I'm not being entirely rational about the situation, but I can't help feeling the way I feel."

"I have some patients to see," Hannaport said, glancing at his watch again. "But let me leave you with one thought that might help you handle this."

"I'd like to hear it."

"The girl suffered only minor physical injuries. I won't say they were negligible injuries, but they were damned close to it. So you've got nothing to feel guilty about on that score. As for her amnesia . . . well, maybe the accident had nothing to do with it."

"Nothing to do with it? But I assumed that when she hit her head on the car or on the pavement—"

"I'm sure you know a blow on the head isn't the only cause of amnesia," Dr. Hannaport said. "It's not even the most common factor in such cases. Stress, emotional shock—they can result in loss of memory. In fact we don't yet understand the human mind well enough to say for sure exactly what causes most cases of amnesia. As far as this girl is concerned, everything points to the conclusion that she was in her current state even before she stepped in front of your car." He emphasized each argument in favor of his theory by raising fingers on his right hand. "One: She wasn't carrying any ID. Two: She was wandering around in the pouring rain without a coat or an umbrella, as if she was in a daze. Three: From what I understand, the witnesses say she was acting very strange before you ever came on the scene." He waggled his three raised fingers. "Three very good reasons why you shouldn't be so eager to blame yourself for the kid's condition."

"Maybe you're right, but I still—"

"I *am* right," he said. "There's no maybe about it. Give yourself a break, Dr. Tracy."

A woman with a sharp, nasal voice paged Dr. Hannaport on the hospital's tinny public address system.

"Thank you for your time," Carol said. "You've been more than kind."

"Come back this evening and talk to the girl if you want. I'm sure you'll find she doesn't blame you one bit."

He turned and hurried across the gaudy lounge, in answer to the page's call; the tails of his white lab coat fluttered behind him.

Carol went to the pay phones and called her office. She explained the situation to her secretary, Thelma, and arranged for the rescheduling of the patients she had intended to see today. Then she dialed home, and Paul answered on the third ring.

"You just caught me as I was going out the door," he said. "I've got to drive down to O'Brian's office and pick up a new set of application papers. Ours were lost in the mess yesterday. So far, this has been a day I should have slept through."

"Ditto on this end," she said.

"What's wrong?"

She told him about the accident and briefly summarized her conversation with Dr. Hannaport.

"It could have been worse," Paul said. "At least we can be thankful no one was killed or crippled."

"That's what everyone keeps telling me: 'It could have been worse, Carol.' But it seems plenty bad enough to me."

"Are you all right?"

"Yeah. I told you. I wasn't even scratched."

"I don't mean physically. I mean, are you together emotionally? You sound shaky."

"I am. Just a little."

"I'll come to the hospital," he said.

"No, no. That's not necessary."

"Are you sure you should drive?"

"I drove here after the accident without trouble, and I'm feeling better now than I did then. I'll be okay. What I'm going to do is, I'm going over to Grace's house. She's only a mile from here; it's easier than going home. I have to sponge off my clothes, dry them out, and press them. I need a shower, too. I'll probably have an early dinner with Grace, if that's all right by her, and then I'll come back here during visiting hours this evening."

"When will you be home?"

"Probably not until eight or eight-thirty."

"I'll miss you."

"Miss you, too."

"Give my best to Grace," he said. "And tell her I think she *is* the next Nostradamus."

"What's that supposed to mean?"

"Grace called a while ago. Said she had two nightmares recently, and you figured in both. She was afraid something was going to happen to you."

"Seriously?"

"Yeah. She was embarrassed about it. Afraid I'd think she was getting senile or something."

"You told her about the lightning yesterday?"

"Yeah. But she felt something else would happen, something bad."

"And it did."

"Creepy, huh?"

"Decidedly," Carol said. She remembered her own nightmare: the black void; the flashing, silvery object drawing nearer, nearer.

"I'm sure Grace'll tell you all about it," Paul said. "And I'll see you this evening."

"I love you," Carol said.

"Love you, too."

She put down the phone and went outside to the parking lot.

Gray-black thunderheads churned across the sky, but only a thin rain was falling now. The wind was still cold and sharp; it sang in the power lines overhead, sounding like a swarm of angry wasps.

●ıı●ıı●

The semiprivate room had two beds, but the second one was not currently in use. At the moment, no nurse was present either. The girl was alone.

She lay under a crisp white sheet and a cream-colored blanket, staring at the acoustic-tile ceiling. She had a headache, and she could feel each dully throbbing, burning cut and abrasion on her battered body, but she knew she was not seriously hurt.

Fear, not pain, was her worst enemy. She was frightened by her inability to remember who she was. On the other hand, she was plagued by the inexplicable yet unshakable feeling that it would be foolish and exceedingly dangerous to remember her past. Without knowing why, she suspected that full remembrance would be the death of her—an odd notion that she found more frightening than anything else.

She knew her amnesia wasn't the result of the accident. She had a misty recollection of walking along the street in the rain a minute or two before she had blundered in front of the Volkswagen. Even then, she had been disoriented, afraid, unable to remember her name, utterly unfamiliar with the strange city in which she found herself and unable to recall how she had gotten there. The thread of her memory definitely had begun unraveling prior to the accident.

She wondered if it was possible that her amnesia was like a shield, protecting her from something horrible in the past. Did forgetfulness somehow equal safety?

Why? Safety from what?

What could I be running from? she asked herself.

She sensed that recovery of her identity was possible. In fact her memories seemed almost within her grasp. She felt as though the past lay at the bottom of a dark hole, close enough to touch; all she had to do was summon sufficient strength and courage to poke her hand into that lightless place and grope for the truth, without fear of what might bite her.

However, when she tried hard to remember, when she probed into that hole, her fear grew and grew until it was no longer just ordinary fear; it became incapacitating terror. Her stomach knotted, and her throat swelled tight, and she broke out in a greasy sweat, and she became so dizzy that she nearly fainted.

On the edge of unconsciousness, she saw and heard something disturbing, alarming—a fuzzy fragment of a dream, a vision—which she couldn't quite identify but which frightened her nonetheless. The vision was composed of a single sound and a single, mysterious image. The image was hypnotic but simple: a quick flash of light, a silvery glimmer from a not-quite-visible object that was swinging back and forth in deep shadows; a gleaming pendulum, perhaps. The sound was hard-edged and threatening but not identifiable, a loud hammering noise, yet more than that.

Thunk! Thunk! Thunk!

She jerked, quivered, as if something had struck her.

Thunk!

She wanted to scream, couldn't.

She realized that her hands were fisted and that they were full of twisted, sweat-soaked sheets.

Thunk!

She stopped trying to remember who she was.

Maybe it's better that I don't know, she thought.

Her heartbeat gradually slowed to normal, and she was able to draw her breath without wheezing. Her stomach unknotted.

The hammering sound faded.

After a while she looked at the window. A flock of large, black birds reeled across the turbulent sky.

What's going to happen to me? she wondered.

Even when the nurse came in to see how she was doing, and even when the doctor joined the nurse a moment later, the girl felt utterly, dishearteningly alone.

5

GRACE'S kitchen smelled of coffee and warm spice cake. Rain washed down the window, obscuring the view of the rose garden that lay behind the house.

"I've never believed in clairvoyance or premonitions."

"Neither have I," Grace said. "But now I wonder. After all, I have two nightmares about you getting hurt, and the next thing I hear is that you've had two close calls, just as if you were acting out a script or something."

They sat at the small table by the kitchen window. Carol was wearing one of Grace's robes and a pair of Grace's slippers while her own clothes finished drying out.

"Only *one* close call," she told Grace. "The lightning. That was a gut-wrencher, all right. But I wasn't really in any danger this morning. That poor girl was the one who nearly got killed."

Grace shook her head. "No. It was a close call for you, too. Didn't you tell me you slid toward the oncoming traffic when you braked to avoid the girl? And didn't you say the Cadillac missed you by an inch or less? Well, what if it *hadn't* missed? If that Caddy had rammed your little VW, you certainly wouldn't have walked away without a scratch."

Frowning, Carol said, "I hadn't looked at it that way."

"You've been so busy worrying about the girl that you haven't had a chance to think about yourself."

Carol ate a bite of spice cake and washed it down with coffee. "You're not the only one having nightmares." She summarized her own dream: the severed heads, the houses that dissolved behind her as she passed through them, the flickering, silvery object.

Grace clasped her hands around her coffee cup and hunched over the table. There was worry in her blue eyes. "That's one nasty dream. What do you make of it?"

"Oh, I don't think it's prophetic."

"Why couldn't it be? Mine appear to have been."

"Yes, but—it doesn't follow that both of us are turning into soothsayers. Besides, my dream didn't make a whole lot of sense. It was just too wild to be taken seriously. I mean, severed heads that suddenly come to life—that sort of thing isn't really going to happen."

"It could be prophetic without being *literally* prophetic. I mean, it might be a symbolic warning."

"Of what?"

"I don't see any easy interpretation of it. But I

really think you ought to be extra careful for a while. God, I know I'm starting to sound like a phony gypsy fortune-teller, like Maria Ouspenskya in all those old monster movies from the thirties, but I still don't think you should dismiss it as just an ordinary dream. Especially not after what's already happened."

●H●II●

Later, after lunch, as Grace squirted some liquid soap into the sinkful of dirty dishes, she said, "How's the situation with the adoption agency? Does it look like they'll give you and Paul a child soon?"

Carol hesitated.

Grace glanced at her. "Something wrong?"

Taking the dish towel from the rack and unfolding it, Carol said, "No. Not really. O'Brian says we'll be approved. It's a sure thing, he says."

"But you're still worried about it."

"A little," Carol admitted.

"Why?"

"I'm not sure. It's just that . . . I've had this feeling. . . ."

"What feeling?"

"That it won't work out."

"Why shouldn't it?"

"I can't shake the idea that somebody's trying to stop us from adopting."

"Who?"

Carol shrugged.

"O'Brian?" Grace asked.

"No, no. He's on our side."

"Someone on the recommendations committee?"

"I don't know. I don't actually have any evidence

of ill will toward Paul and me. I can't point my finger at anyone."

Grace washed some silverware, put it in the drainage rack, and said, "You've wanted to adopt for so long that you can't believe it's finally happening, so you're looking for boogeymen where there aren't any."

"Maybe."

"You're just spooked because of the lightning yesterday and the accident this morning."

"Maybe."

"That's understandable. It spooks me, too. But the adoption will go through as smooth as can be."

"I hope so," Carol said. But she thought about the lost set of application forms, and she wondered.

●‖●‖●

By the time Paul got back from the adoption agency, the rain had stopped, though the wind was still cold and damp.

He got the ladder out of the garage and climbed onto the least slanted portion of the many-angled roof. The wet shingles squeaked under his feet as he moved cautiously across the slope toward the television antenna, which was anchored near a brick chimney.

His legs were rubbery. He suffered from a mild case of acrophobia, a fear that had never become incapacitating because he occasionally forced himself to challenge and overcome it, as he was doing now.

When he reached the chimney, he put a hand against it for support and looked out across the roofs of the neighboring homes. The storm-dark September sky had settled lower, lower, until it appeared to be only six or eight feet above the tallest houses. He felt as if he could raise his arm and rap his knuckles on the bellies of the clouds, eliciting a hard, ironlike *clank*.

He crouched with his back to the chimney and inspected the TV antenna. The brace-plate was held down by four bolts that went through the shingles, either directly into a roof beam or into a stud linking two beams. None of the bolts was missing. None of them was loose. The plate was firmly attached to the house, and the antenna was anchored securely to the plate. The antenna could not possibly have been responsible for the hammering sound that had shaken the house.

●II●II●

After washing the dishes, Grace and Carol went into the study. The room reeked of cat urine and feces. Aristophanes had made his toilet on the seat of the big easy chair.

Stunned, Grace said, "I don't believe it. Ari *always* uses the litter box like he's supposed to do. He's never done anything like this before."

"He's always been a fussy cat, hasn't he? Fastidious."

"Exactly. But now look what he's done. That chair'll have to be reupholstered. I guess I'd better find the silly beast, put his nose to this mess, and give him a good scolding. I don't want this to become a habit, for God's sake."

They looked in every room, but they couldn't find Aristophanes. Apparently, he had slipped out of the house by way of the pet door in the kitchen.

Returning to the study with Grace, Carol said, "Earlier, you mentioned something about Ari tearing up a few things."

Grace winced. "Yes. I didn't want to have to tell you—but he shredded two of those lovely little needlepoint pillows you made for me. I was sick about it. After all the work you put into those, and then he just—"

"Don't worry about it," Carol said. "I'll make you a couple of new pillows. I enjoy doing it. Needlepoint relaxes me. I only asked because I thought maybe, if Ari's been doing a lot of things that're out of character, it might be a sign that he isn't well."

Grace frowned. "He, *looks* healthy. His coat's glossy, and he's certainly as spry as ever."

"Animals are like people in some ways. And when a person suddenly starts behaving strangely, that *can* be an indication of a physical malady, anything from a brain tumor to an imbalanced diet."

"I suppose I ought to take him to the vet."

Carol said, "While there's a break in the rain, why don't we go outside and see if we can find him?"

"Wasted effort. When a cat doesn't want to be found, it *won't* be found. Besides, he'll come back by dinnertime. I'll keep him in all night, and take him to the vet's in the morning." Grace looked at the mess on the easy chair, grimaced, and shook her head. "This isn't like my Ari," she said worriedly. "It's just not like him at all."

●ıı●ıı●

The number on the open door was 316.

Hesitantly, Carol stepped into the white and blue hospital room and stopped just past the threshold. The place smelled vaguely of Lysol.

The girl was sitting up in the bed nearest the window, her face averted from the door, staring out at the twilight-shrouded hospital grounds. She turned her head when she realized she was no longer alone, and when she looked at Carol there was no recognition in her blue-gray eyes.

"May I come in?" Carol asked.

"Sure."

Carol went to the foot of the bed. "How are you feeling?"

"Okay."

"With all the scrapes and cuts and bruises, it must be hard to get comfortable."

"Gee, I'm not banged up all that bad. I'm just a little sore. It's nothing that's going to kill me. Everyone's so nice; you're all making too much of a fuss about me."

"How's your head feel?"

"I had a headache when I first came to, but it's been gone for hours."

"Double vision?"

"Nothing like that," the girl said. A strand of golden hair slipped from behind her ear and fell across her cheek; she tucked it back in place. "Are you a doctor?"

"Yes," Carol said. "My name's Carol Tracy."

"You can call me Jane. That's the name on my chart. Jane Doe. I guess it's as good as any. It might even turn out to be a lot nicer than my real name. Maybe I'm actually Zelda or Myrtle or something like that." She had a lovely smile. "You're the umpteenth doctor who's been in to see me. How many do I have, anyway?"

"I'm not one of yours," Carol said. "I'm here because ... well... it was my car you stepped in front of."

"Oh. Hey, gee, I'm awfully sorry. I hope there wasn't a lot of damage."

Surprised by the girl's statement and by the genuine look of concern on her face, Carol laughed. "For heaven's sake, honey, don't worry about my car. It's your health that's important, not the VW. And *I'm* the one who should be apologizing. I feel terrible about this."

"You shouldn't," the girl said. "I still have all my teeth, and none of my bones are broken, and Dr. Hannaport says the boys will still be interested in me." She grinned self-consciously.

"He's certainly right about the boys," Carol said. "You're a very pretty girl."

The grin became a shy smile, and the girl looked down at the covers on her lap, blushing.

Carol said, "I was hoping I'd find you here with your folks."

The girl tried to maintain a cheerful facade, but when she looked up, fear and doubt showed through the mask. "I guess they haven't filed a missing-persons report yet. But it's only a matter of time."

"Have you remembered anything at all about your past?"

"Not yet. But I will." She straightened the collar of her hospital gown and smoothed the covers over her lap as she talked. "Dr. Hannaport says everything'll probably come back to me if I just don't push too hard at remembering. He says I'm lucky I don't have global amnesia. That's when you even forget how to read and write. I'm not *that* bad off! Heck, no. Boy, wouldn't that be something? What if I had to learn to read, write, add, subtract, multiply, divide, and spell all over again? What a bore!" She finished smoothing her covers and looked up again. "Anyway, I'll most likely have my memory back in a day or two."

"I'm sure you will," Carol said, though she wasn't sure at all. "Is there anything you need?"

"No. They supply everything. Even tiny tubes of toothpaste."

"What about books, magazines?"

The girl sighed. "I was bored out of my skull this afternoon. You think they might keep a pile of old magazines for the patients?"

"Probably. What do you like to read?"

"Everything. I *love* to read; I remember that much. But I can't remember the titles of any books or magazines. This amnesia sure is funny, isn't it?"

"Hilarious," Carol said. "Sit tight. I'll be right back."

At the nurses' station at the end of the hall, she explained who she was and arranged to rent a small television set for Jane Doe's room. An orderly promised to hook it up right away.

The chief RN on duty—a stocky, gray-haired woman who wore her glasses on a chain around her neck—said, "She's such a sweet girl. She's charmed everyone. Hasn't complained or uttered a cross word to a soul. There aren't many teenagers with her composure."

Carol took the elevator down to the ground-floor lobby and went to the newsstand. She bought a Hershey bar, an Almond Joy, and six magazines that looked as if they would appeal to a young girl. By the time she got back to room 316, the orderly had just finished installing the TV.

"You shouldn't have done all this," the girl said.

"When my parents show up, I'll make sure they pay you back."

"I won't accept a dime," Carol said.

"But—"

"No buts."

"I don't need to be pampered. I'm fine. Really. If you—"

"I'm not pampering you, honey. Just think of the magazines and the television as forms of therapy. In fact, they might be precisely the tools you need to break through this amnesia."

"What do you mean?"

"Well, if you watch enough television, you might see a show you remember seeing before. That might spark a sort of chain reaction of memories."

"You think so?"

"It's better than just sitting and staring at the walls or out the window. Nothing in this place is going to spark a memory because none of it is related to your past. But there's a chance the TV will do the trick."

The girl picked up the remote-control device that the orderly had given her, and she switched on the television set. A popular situation comedy was on.

"Familiar?" Carol asked.

The girl shook her head: no. Tears glistened in the corners of her eyes.

"Hey, don't get upset," Carol said. "It would be amazing if you remembered the first thing you saw. It's bound to take time."

She nodded and bit her lip, trying not to cry.

Carol moved close, took the girl's hand; it was cool.

"Will you come back tomorrow?" Jane asked shakily.

"Of course I will."

"I mean, if it's not out of your way."

"It's no trouble at all."

"Sometimes . . ."

"What?"

The girl shuddered. "Sometimes I'm so afraid."

"Don't be afraid, honey. Please don't. It'll all work out. You'll see. You're going to be back on the track in no time," Carol said, wishing she could think of something more reassuring than those few hollow platitudes. But she knew her inadequate response was occasioned by her own nagging doubts.

The girl pulled a tissue out of the Kleenex dispenser that was built into the side of the tall metal nightstand. She blew her nose, used another tissue to daub at her eyes. She had slumped down in the bed; now she sat up straight, lifted her chin, squared her slender shoulders, and readjusted her covers. When she looked up at Carol, she was smiling again. "Sorry," she said. "I don't know what got into me. Being a crybaby isn't going to solve anything. Anyway, you're right. My folks will probably show up tomorrow, and everything'll work out for the best. Look, Dr. Tracy, if you come to see me tomorrow—"

"I will."

"If you do, promise not to bring me any more candy or magazines or anything. Okay? There's no reason for you to spend your money like that. You've already done too much for me. Besides, the best thing you could do is just come. I mean, it's nice to know someone outside the hospital cares about me. It's nice to know I haven't been lost or forgotten in here. Oh, sure, the nurses and the doctors are swell. They really are, and I'm grateful. They care about me, but it's sort of their job to care. You know? So that's not exactly the same thing, is it?" She laughed nervously. "Am I making sense?"

"I know exactly what you're feeling," Carol assured her. She was achingly aware of the girl's profound loneliness, for she had been lonely and frightened when she was the same age, before Grace Mitowski had taken custody of her and had given her large measures of guidance and love.

She stayed with Jane until visiting hours were over. Before she left, she planted a motherly kiss on the girl's forehead, and it seemed like a perfectly natural thing to do. A bond had formed between them in a surprisingly short time.

Outside, in the hospital parking lot, the sodium-vapor lights leached the true colors from the cars and made them all look yellowish.

The night was chilly. No rain had fallen during the afternoon or evening, but the air was heavy, damp. Thunder rumbled in the distance, and a new storm appeared to be on the way.

She sat for a moment behind the wheel of the VW, staring up at the third-floor window of the girl's room.

"What a terrific kid," she said aloud.

She felt that someone quite special had come unexpectedly into her life.

● ‖ ● ‖ ●

Near midnight, a river-cold wind came out of the west and made the trees dance. The starless, moonless, utterly lightless night pressed close around the house and seemed to Grace to be a living thing; it snuffled at the doors and windows.

Rain began to fall.

She went to bed as the hall clock was striking twelve, and twenty minutes later she began to drift over the edge of sleep as if she were a leaf borne by cool currents toward a great waterfall. On the brink, with only darkness churning under her, she heard movement in the bedroom and instantly came awake again.

A series of stealthy sounds. A soft scrape. A rattle that died even as it began. A silken rustle.

She sat up, heart quickening, and opened the night-stand drawer. With one hand she felt blindly for the .22 pistol she kept in the drawer, and with the other hand she groped silently for the lamp switch. She touched the gun and lamp at the same moment.

With light, the source of the noise was clearly visible. Ari was crouched atop the highboy, staring down at her, as if he had been about to spring onto the bed.

"What are you doing in here? You know the rules."

He blinked but didn't move. His muscles were bunched and taut; his fur was standing up on the back of his neck.

For sanitary reasons, she would allow him to climb neither onto the kitchen counters nor into her bed; generally, she kept the master bedroom door firmly shut, day and night, rather than tempt him. Already, housecleaning required extra hours each week because of him, for she was determined that the air should not contain even the slightest trace of cat odor; likewise, she was not about to subject her visitors to furniture covered with loose animal hairs. She loved Ari, and she thought him fine company, and for the most part she gave him the run of the house in spite of the extra work he caused her. But she was not prepared to live with cat hairs in her food or in her sheets.

She got out of bed, stepped into her slippers.

Ari watched.

"Come down from there this instant," Grace said, looking up at him with her sternest expression.

His shining eyes were gas-flame blue.

Grace went to the bedroom door, opened it, stepped out of the way, and said, "Shoo."

The cat's muscles relaxed. He slumped in a furry puddle atop the highboy, as if his bones had melted. He yawned and began to lick one of his black paws.

"Hey!" she said.

Aristophanes raised his head languidly, peered down at her.

"Out," she said gruffly. "Now."

When he still didn't move, she started toward the highboy, and he was at last encouraged to obey. He jumped down and darted past her so fast she didn't have time to swat him. He went into the hall, and she closed the door.

In bed again, with the lights out, she remembered the way he had looked as he perched atop the highboy: facing her, *aimed* at her, shoulders drawn up, head held low, haunches tense, his fur electrified, his eyes bright and slightly demented. He had intended to jump onto the bed and scare the bejesus out of her; there was no doubt about that. But such schemes were a kitten's games; Ari had not been playful in that fashion for the past three or four years, ever since he had attained a rather indolent maturity. What on earth had gotten into him?

That settles it, she told herself. We'll pay a visit to the veterinarian first thing in the morning. Good Lord, I might have a schizophrenic cat on my hands!

Seeking rest, she let the night embrace her again. She allowed herself to be carried along by the riverlike sound of the soughing wind. Within a few minutes she was once more being borne toward the waterfall of sleep. She trembled on the edge of it, and a quiver of uneasiness passed through her, a chill that nearly broke the spell, but then she dropped down into darkness.

She dreamed that she was trekking across a vast underwater landscape of brilliantly colored coral and seaweed and strange, undulating plants. A cat lurked among the plants, a big one, much bigger than a tiger, but with the coloring of a Siamese. It was stalking her. She could see its saucer eyes peering at her through the murky sea, from among wavering stalks of marine vegetation. She could hear and feel its low purr transmitted by the water. She paused repeatedly during her suboceanic trek so that she could fill a series of yellow bowls with generous portions of Meow Mix in the hope of pacifying the cat, but she knew in her heart that the beast would not be content until it had sunk its claws into her. She moved steadily past towers of coral, past grottoes, across wide aquatic plains of shifting sand, waiting for the cat to snarl and lunge from concealment, waiting for it to rip open her face and gouge out her eyes. . . .

Once, she woke and thought she heard Aristophanes scratching insistently on the other side of the closed bedroom door. But she was groggy and couldn't trust her senses; she wasn't able to wrench herself fully awake, and in a few seconds she sank down into the dream once more.

❂‖❂‖❂

At one o'clock in the morning, the third floor of the hospital was so quiet that Harriet Gilbey, the head nurse on the graveyard shift, felt as though she was deep underground, in some kind of military complex, tucked into the stony roots of a mountain, far from the real world and the background noises of real life. The only sounds were the whisper of the heating system and the occasional squeak of the nurses' rubber-soled shoes on the highly polished tile floors.

Harriet—a small, pretty, neatly uniformed black woman—was at the nurses' station, around the corner from the bank of elevators, entering data on patients' charts, when the tranquility of the third floor was abruptly shattered by a piercing scream. She moved out from behind the reception desk and hurried along the hall, following the shrill cry. It came from room 316. When Harriet pushed open the door, stepped into the room, and snapped on the overhead lights, the screaming stopped as suddenly as it had begun.

The girl they called Jane Doe was in bed, flat on her back, one arm raised and angled across her face as if she were warding off a blow, the other hand hooked on to one of the safety rails. She had kicked the sheets and the blanket into a tangled wad at the foot of the bed, and her hospital gown was rucked up over her hips. She tossed her head violently from side

to side, gasping, pleading with an imaginary assailant:
"No . . . no . . . no. Don't! Please don't kill me! *No!*"

With gentle hands, a gentle voice, and patient insistence, Harriet tried to quiet the girl. At first Jane resisted all ministrations. She had been given a sedative earlier. Now she was having trouble waking up. Gradually, however, she shook off the nightmare and calmed down.

Another nurse, Kay Hamilton, appeared at Harriet's side. "What happened? Must've woke up half the floor."

"Just a bad dream," Harriet said.

Jane blinked sleepily at them. "She was trying to kill me."

"Hush now," Harriet said. "It was only a dream. No one here will hurt you."

"A dream?" Jane asked, her voice slurred. "Oh. Yeah. Just a dream. Whew! What a dream."

The girl's thin white gown and the tangled sheets were damp with perspiration. Harriet and Kay replaced them with fresh linens.

As soon as the bed had been changed, Jane succumbed to the lingering tug of the sedative. She turned onto her side and murmured happily in her sleep; she even smiled.

"Looks like she switched to a better channel," Harriet said.

"Poor kid. After what she's been through, the least she deserves is a good night's sleep."

They watched her for a minute, then left the room, turning off the lights and closing the door.

Alone, deep in sleep, transported into a different dream from the one that had elicited her screams, Jane sighed, smiled, giggled quietly.

"The ax," she whispered in her sleep. "The ax. Oh, the ax. Yes. Yes."

Her hands curled slightly, as if she were clutching a solid but invisible object.

"The ax," she whispered, and the second of those two words reverberated softly through the dark room.

●‖●‖●

Thunk!

Carol ran through the huge living room, across the oriental carpet, banging her hip against the edge of the credenza.

Thunk! Thunk!

She dashed through the archway, into a long hall, headed toward the stairs that led to the second floor. When she glanced behind her, she saw that the house had vanished in her wake and had been replaced by a pitch-black void in which something silvery flickered back and forth, back and forth....

Thunk!

Understanding came with a flash; she knew what the glimmering object was. An ax. The blade of an ax. Glinting as it swung from side to side.

Thunk ... thunk-thunk ...

Whimpering, she climbed the stairs toward the second floor.

Thunk ... thunk ...

At times the blade seemed to be biting into wood; the sound of it was dry, splintery. But at other times the sound had a subtly different quality, as if the blade were slicing brutally into a substance much softer than wood, into something wet and tender.

Into flesh?

Thunk!

Carol groaned in her sleep, turned restlessly, flinging off the sheets.

Then she was running across the high meadow. The trees ahead. The void behind. And the ax. The ax.

6

FRIDAY morning, there was another break in the rain, but the day was dressed in fog. The light coming through the hospital window was wintry, bleak.

Jane had only a hazy recollection of the nurses changing her sheets and her sweat-soaked bed gown during the night. She vaguely recalled having a frightening dream, too, but she couldn't bring to mind a single detail of it.

She was still unable to remember her name or anything else about herself. She could cast her mind back as far as the accident yesterday morning, perhaps even to a point a minute or so on the other side of the accident, but beyond that there was only a blank wall where her past should have been.

During breakfast, she read an article in one of the magazines that Carol Tracy had bought for her. Although there were no visiting hours until this afternoon, Jane was already looking forward to seeing the woman again. Dr. Hannaport and the nurses were nice, every one of them, but none of them affected her as positively as Carol Tracy did. For reasons she could not understand, she felt more secure, more at ease, less frightened by her amnesia when she was with Dr. Tracy than when she was with the others. Maybe that was what people meant when they said a doctor had a good bedside manner.

●ll●ll●

Shortly after nine o'clock, when Paul was on the freeway, headed downtown to deliver the new set of application papers to Alfred O'Brian's office, the Pontiac's engine cut out. It didn't sputter or cough; the pistons simply stopped firing while the car was hurtling along at nearly fifty miles an hour. As the Pontiac's speed plummeted, its power steering began to freeze up. Traffic whizzed past on both sides at sixty and sixty-five, faster than the speed limit, too fast for the misty weather. Paul maneuvered the car across two lanes, toward the right-hand shoulder of the road. Second by second, he expected to hear a short squeal of brakes and feel the sickening impact of another car against his, but amazingly, he was able to avoid a collision. Wrestling with the stiffening steering wheel, he brought the Pontiac to a full stop on the berm.

He leaned back in his seat and closed his eyes until he had regained his composure. When at last he leaned forward and twisted the key in the ignition, the starter didn't make the slightest response; the battery had no juice to offer. He tried a few more times, then gave up.

A freeway exit was just ahead, and there was a service station less than a block from the off-ramp. Paul walked to it in ten minutes.

The station was busy, and the owner couldn't spare his young assistant—a big, redheaded, open-faced kid named Corky—until the stream of customers subsided to a trickle shortly before ten o'clock. Then Paul and Corky rode back to the crippled Pontiac in a tow truck.

They tried jump-starting the car, but the battery wouldn't hold a charge. The Pontiac had to be towed back to the station.

Corky intended to replace the battery and have the car running in half an hour. But it wasn't the battery after all, and the estimated time for completion of the repairs was extended again and again. Finally, Corky found a problem with the electrical system and fixed it.

Paul was stranded for three hours, always sure he would be on his way in just another twenty or thirty minutes. But it was one-thirty when he finally parked the revitalized Pontiac in front of the adoption agency's offices.

Alfred O'Brian came out to the reception lounge to greet Paul. He was wearing a well-tailored brown suit, a neatly pressed, cream-colored shirt, a neatly arranged, beige display handkerchief in the breast pocket of his suit jacket, and a pair of neatly shined, brown wing-tip shoes. He accepted the application, but he wasn't optimistic about the possibility of making all the required verifications prior to the recommendations committee's meeting next Wednesday morning.

"We'll try to do a rush job on your papers," he told Paul. "I owe you that much at least! But in getting these verifications, we have to deal with people outside this office, and some of them won't get back to us right away or won't like being hurried. It always takes a minimum of three full business days to run a complete verification, sometimes four or five days, sometimes even longer, so I very much doubt that we'll be ready for this session of the recommendations committee, even though I want to be. We'll probably have to submit your application at the second September meeting, at the end of the month. I feel terrible about that, Mr. Tracy. I'm more sorry than I can say. I truly am. If we hadn't lost those papers in the turmoil yesterday—"

"Don't worry about it," Paul said. "The lightning wasn't your doing, and neither was the problem with my car. Carol and I have waited a long, long time to adopt a child. Another two weeks isn't much in the scheme of things."

"When your papers *are* presented to the committee, you'll be approved quickly," O'Brian said. "I've never been more sure about a couple than I am about you. That's what I'm going to tell them."

"I appreciate that," Paul said.

"If we can't make Wednesday's meeting—and I assure you we'll try our best—then it's only a minor, temporary setback. Nothing to be concerned about. Just a bit of bad luck."

●||●||●

Dr. Brad Templeton was a fine veterinarian. However, to Grace, he always looked out of place when he was ministering to a cat or dog. He was a big man who would have looked more at home treating horses and farm animals in a country practice, where his massive shoulders and muscular arms would be of more use. He stood six-five, weighed about two hundred and twenty pounds, and had a ruddy, rugged, but pleasing face. When he plucked Aristophanes out of the padded travel basket, the cat looked like a toy in his enormous hands.

"He looks fit," Brad said, putting Ari on the stainless-steel table that stood in the middle of the sparkling clean surgery.

"He's never been one to tear up the furniture, not since he was just a kitten," Grace said. "He's never been a climber, either. But now, every time I turn around, he's perched on top of something, peering down at me."

Brad examined Ari, feeling for swollen glands and enlarged joints. The cat cooperated docilely, even when Brad used a rectal thermometer on him. "Temperature's normal."

"*Something's* wrong," Grace insisted.

Aristophanes purred, rolled onto his back, asking for his belly to be rubbed.

Brad rubbed him and was rewarded with an even louder purr. "Is he off his food?"

"No," Grace said. "He stills eats well."

"Vomiting?"

"No."

"Diarrhea?"

"No. He hasn't shown any symptoms like those.

It's just that he's...different. He's not at all like he was. Every symptom I can point to is a symptom of a *personality* change, not an indication of physical deterioration. Like destroying the pillows. Leaving the mess on the armchair. The sudden interest he's taken in climbing. And he's gotten very sneaky lately, always creeping around, hiding·from me, watching me when he thinks I don't see him."

"All cats are a bit sneaky," Brad said, frowning. "That's the nature of the beast."

"Ari didn't used to sneak," Grace said. "Not like he's been doing the last couple of days. And he's not as friendly as he used to be. The last two days, he hasn't wanted to be petted or cuddled."

Still frowning, Brad lifted his gaze from the cat and met Grace's eyes. "But dear, look at him."

Ari was still on his back, getting his belly rubbed, and clearly relishing all the attention being directed at him. His tail swished back and forth across the steel table. He raised one paw and batted playfully at the doctor's large, leathery hand.

Sighing, Grace said, "I know what you're thinking. I'm an old woman. Old women get funny ideas."

"No, no, no. I wasn't thinking any such thing."

"Old women become obsessively attached to their pets because sometimes their pets are the only company they have, their only real friends."

"I am perfectly aware that doesn't apply to you, Grace. Not with all the friends you've got in this town. I merely—"

She smiled and patted his cheek. "Don't protest too strongly, Brad. I know what's going through your mind. Some old women are so afraid of losing their pets that they think they see signs of illness where there are none. Your reaction is understandable. It doesn't offend me. It *does* frustrate me because I know something *is* wrong with Ari."

Brad looked down at the cat again, continued stroking its belly, and said, "Have you changed his diet in any way?"

"No. He gets the same brand of cat food, at the same times of day, in the same quantities he's always gotten it."

"Has the company changed the product recently?"

"How do you mean?"

"Well, does the package say 'new, improved,' or 'richer flavor,' or anything like that?"

She thought about it for a moment, then shook her head. "I don't think so."

"Sometimes, when they change a formula, they add a new preservative or a new artificial flavoring or coloring agent, and some pets have an allergic reaction to it."

"But wouldn't that be a physical reaction? Like I said, this seems to be strictly a personality change."

Brad nodded. "I'm sure you know food additives can cause behavioral problems in some children. A lot of hyperactive kids calm down when they're put on a diet free of the major additives. Animals can be affected by these things, too. From what you've told me, it sounds like Aristophanes is intermittently hyperactive and may be responding to a subtle change in the formulation of his cat food. Switch him to another brand, wait a week for his system to purge itself of whatever additives have offended it, and he'll probably be the old Ari again."

"If he isn't?"

"Then bring him in, leave him with me for a couple

of days, and I'll give him a really thorough going over. But I strongly recommend that we try changing his diet first, before we go to all that trouble and expense."

You *are* humoring me, Grace thought. Just coddling an old lady.

"Very well," she said. "I'll try changing his food. But if he's still not himself a week from now, I'll want you to give him a complete battery of tests."

"Of course."

"I'll want an answer."

On the stainless-steel table, Aristophanes purred, happily twitched his long tail, and looked infuriatingly *normal*.

●‖●‖●

Later, at home, just inside the front door, when Grace slipped the latch on the padded travel basket and opened the lid, Aristophanes exploded out of confinement with a hiss and a snarl, his fur bristling, his ears laid back against his head, eyes wild. He clawed her hand and squealed as she thrust him away from her. He sprinted down the hall, disappeared into the kitchen, where the pet door gave him access to the rear yard.

Shocked, Grace stared at her hand. Ari's claws had made three short furrows in the meaty edge of her palm. Blood welled up and began to trickle down her wrist.

●‖●‖●

Carol's last appointment on Friday was at one o'clock: a fifty-minute session with Kathy Lombino, a fifteen-

year-old girl who was gradually recovering from anorexia nervosa. Five months ago, when she had first
been brought to Carol, Kathy had weighed only sev-
enty-five pounds, at least thirty pounds below her
ideal weight. She had been teetering on the edge of
starvation, repelled by the sight and even the thought
of food, stubbornly refusing to eat more than an occasional soda cracker or slice of bread, often gagging
on even those bland morsels. When she was put in
front of a mirror and forced to confront the pathetic
sight of her emaciated body, she still berated herself
for being fat and could not be convinced that she was,
in fact, frighteningly thin. Her prospects for survival
had seemed slight. Now she weighed ninety pounds,
up fifteen, still well below a healthy weight for a girl
of her height and bone structure, but at least she was
no longer in danger of dying. A loss of self-respect
and self-confidence was nearly always the seed from
which anorexia nervosa grew, and Kathy was beginning to like herself again, a sure sign that she was on
her way back from the brink. She hadn't yet regained
a normal appetite; she still experienced mild revulsion
at the sight and taste of food; but her attitude was far
better than it had been, for now she recognized the
need for food, even though she didn't have any desire
for it. The girl had a long way to go before she would
be fully recovered, but the worst was past for her; in
time she would learn to enjoy food again, and she
would gain weight more rapidly than she had done
thus far, stabilizing around a hundred and five or a
hundred and ten pounds. Kathy's progress had been
immensely satisfying to Carol, and today's session
only added to that satisfaction. As had become cus-
tomary, she and the girl hugged each other at the end
of the session, and Kathy held on tighter and longer

than usual. When the girl left the office, she was smiling.

A few minutes later, at two o'clock, Carol went to the hospital. In the gift shop off the lobby, she bought a deck of playing cards and a miniature checkerboard with nickle-sized checkers that all fit neatly into a vinyl carrying case.

Upstairs, in 316, the television was on, and Jane was reading a magazine. She looked up when Carol entered, and she said, "You really came."

"Said I would, didn't I?"

"What've you got?"

"Cards, checkers. I thought maybe they'd help you pass the time."

"You promised you wouldn't buy me anything else."

"Hey, did I say I was *giving* these to you? No way. You think I'm a soft touch or something? I'm *lending* them, kid. I expect them back. And whenever you return them, they'd better be in as good condition as they are now, or I'll take you all the way to the Supreme Court to get compensated for the damage."

Jane grinned. "Boy, you're tough."

"I eat nails for breakfast."

"Don't they get stuck in your teeth?"

"I pluck 'em out with pliers."

"Ever eat barbed wire?"

"Never for breakfast. I have it for lunch now and then."

They both laughed, and Carol said, "So do you play checkers?"

"I don't know. I don't remember."

"Cards?"

The girl shrugged.

"Nothing's come back yet?" Carol asked.

"Not a thing."

"Don't worry. It will."

"My folks haven't shown up, either."

"Well, you've only been missing for one day. Give them time to find you. It's too soon to start worrying about that."

They played three games of checkers. Jane remembered all of the rules, but she couldn't recall where or with whom she had played before.

The afternoon passed quickly, and Carol enjoyed every minute of it. Jane was charming, bright, and blessed with a good sense of humor. Whether the game was checkers, hearts, or five-hundred rummy, she played to win, but she never pouted when she lost. She was very good company.

The girl's charm and pleasing personality made it highly unlikely that she would go unclaimed for long. Some teenagers are so self-centered, spaced out on drugs, bullheaded, and destructive that when one of them decides to run away from home, his decision often elicits only a sigh of relief from his mother and father. But when a good kid like Jane Doe disappears, a lot of people start sounding alarms.

There must be a family that loves her, Carol thought. They're probably crazy with worry right now. Sooner or later they'll turn up, crying and laughing with relief that their girl has been found alive. So why not sooner? Where *are* they?

●‖●‖●

The doorbell rang at precisely three-thirty. Paul answered it and found a pallid, gray-eyed man of about fifty. He wore gray slacks, a pale gray shirt, and a dark gray sweater.

"Mr. Tracy?"

"Yes. Are you from Safe Homes?"

"That's right," the gray man said. "Name's Bill Alsgood. I *am* Safe Homes. Started the company two years ago."

They shook hands, and Alsgood entered the foyer, looking with interest at the interior of the house. "Lovely place. You're lucky to get same-day service. Usually, I'm scheduled three days in advance. But when you called this morning and said it was an emergency, I'd just had a cancellation."

"You're a building inspector?" Paul asked, closing the door.

"Structural engineer, to be precise. What our company does is inspect the house before it's sold, usually on behalf of the buyer, at his expense. We tell him if he's buying into a heartache of any sort—a leaky roof, a cellar that floods, a crumbling foundation, faulty wiring, bad plumbing, that kind of thing. We're fully bonded, so even if we overlook something, our client is protected. Are you the buyer or the seller?"

"Neither," Paul said. "My wife and I own the place, but we aren't ready to sell it. We're having a problem with the house, and I can't pinpoint the cause of it. I thought you might be able to help."

Alsgood raised one gray eyebrow. "May I suggest that what you need is a good handyman. He'd be considerably cheaper, and once he'd found the trouble, he could fix it, too. We don't do any repair work, you know. We only inspect."

"I'm aware of that. I'm pretty handy myself, but I haven't figured out what's wrong or how to fix it.

I think I need the kind of expert advice that no handyman can give me."

"You *do* know we charge two hundred and fifty dollars for an inspection?"

"I know," Paul said. "But this is an extremely annoying problem, and it might be causing serious structural damage."

"What is it?"

Paul told him about the hammering sounds that occasionally shook the house.

"That's peculiar as hell," Alsgood said. "I've never heard a complaint like it before." He thought for a moment, then said, "Where's your furnace?"

"In the cellar."

"Maybe it's a heating duct problem. Unlikely. But we can start down there and work our way up to the roof until we've found the cause."

For the next two hours, Alsgood looked into every cranny of the house, poked and probed and rapped and visually inspected every inch of the interior, then every inch of the roof, while Paul tagged along, assisting wherever he could. A light rain began to fall when they were still on the roof, and they were both soaked by the time they finished the job and climbed down. Alsgood's left foot slipped off the last rung of the ladder, just as he was about to step onto the waterlogged lawn, and he twisted his ankle painfully. All that risk and inconvenience was for nothing because Alsgood didn't find anything out of the ordinary.

At five-thirty, in the kitchen, they warmed up with coffee while Alsgood filled out his report. Wet and bedraggled, he looked even more pallid than when Paul had first seen him. The rain had transformed his gray clothes—once a variety of shades—into a single, dull hue, so that he appeared to be wearing a drab uniform. "It's basically a solid house, Mr. Tracy. The condition is really topnotch."

"Then where the devil did that sound come from? And why was the whole house shaken by it?"

"I wish I'd heard it."

"I was sure it'd start up at least once while you were here."

Alsgood sipped his coffee, but the warm brew added no color to his cheeks. "Structurally, there's not a thing wrong with this house. That's what my report will say, and I'd stake my reputation on it."

"Which puts me right back at square one," Paul said, folding his hands around his coffee cup.

"I'm sorry you spent all this money without getting an answer," Alsgood said. "I really feel bad about that."

"It isn't your fault. I'm convinced you did a thorough job. In fact, if I ever buy another house, I'll definitely want you to inspect it first. At least I now know the trouble isn't structural, which rules out possibilities and narrows the field of inquiry."

"Maybe you won't even hear it again. It might stop just as suddenly as it started."

"Somehow, I suspect you're wrong about that," Paul said.

Later, at the front door, as Alsgood was leaving, he said, "One thought has occurred to me, but I hesitate to mention it."

"Why?"

"You might think it's off the wall."

"Mr. Alsgood, I'm a desperate man. I'm willing to consider anything, no matter how farfetched it might be."

Alsgood looked at the ceiling, then at the floor, then back along the hall that lay behind Paul, then down at his own feet. "A ghost," he said quietly.

Paul stared at him, surprised.

Alsgood cleared his throat nervously, shifted his eyes to the floor again, then finally raised them and met Paul's gaze. "Maybe you don't believe in ghosts."

"Do you?" Paul asked.

"Yes. I've been interested in the subject most of my life. I have a large collection of publications dealing with spiritualism of all sorts. I've had some personal experiences in haunted houses, too."

"You've seen a ghost?"

"I believe I have, yes, on four occasions. Ectoplasmic apparitions. Insubstantial, manlike shapes drifting in the air. I've also twice witnessed poltergeist phenomena. As far as this house is concerned..." His voice trailed away, and he licked his lips nervously. "If you find this boring or preposterous, I don't want to waste your time."

"Quite frankly," Paul said, "I can't picture myself calling an exorcist in to deal with this. But I'm not entirely close-minded where ghosts are concerned. I find it hard to accept, but I'm certainly willing to listen."

"Reasonable enough," Alsgood said. For the first time since he had rung the doorbell more than two hours ago, color rose into his milky complexion, and his watery eyes brightened with a spark of enthusiasm. "All right. Here's something to consider. From what you've told me, I'd say there might be a poltergeist at work here. Of course, no objects have been hurled around by an unseen presence; there's been no breakage, and poltergeists dearly love to break things. But the shaking of the house, the clattering pots and pans, the little bottles clinking against one another in the spice rack—those are all indications of a poltergeist at work, one that's just beginning to test its powers. If it *is* a poltergeist, then you can expect worse to come. Oh, yes. Definitely. Furniture moving across the floor all by itself. Pictures flung off the walls, lamps knocked down and broken. Dishes flying around the room as if they were birds." His wan countenance flushed with excitement as he considered the supernatural destruction. "Levitations of heavy objects like sofas and beds and refrigerators. Now mind you, there *are* some recorded cases of people being plagued by *benign* poltergeists that don't break much of anything, but the overwhelming number of them are malign, and that's what you'll most likely have to deal with—if indeed you've got one here at all." Having warmed to his subject, he finished in an almost breathless rush of words: "In its most active form, even a benign poltergeist can completely disrupt a household, interfere with your sleep, and keep you so on edge that you don't know whether you're coming or going."

Startled by Alsgood's passionately delivered speech and by the odd new light in the man's eyes, Paul said, "Well...uh...it's really not that bad. Not nearly that bad. Just a hammering sound and—"

"It's not that bad *yet*," Alsgood said somberly. "But if you have a poltergeist here, the situation could deteriorate rapidly. If you've never seen one in action, Mr. Tracy, you simply can't understand what it's like."

Paul was disconcerted by the change in the man. He felt as if he had opened the door to one of those wholesome-looking types who turned out to be pushing crackpot religious pamphlets and who proclaimed the imminence of Judgment Day in the same bubbly, upbeat tone of voice that Donny Osmond might use to introduce his cute little sister, Marie, to a panting audience of Osmond fans. There was a disquieting zeal in Alsgood's manner.

"If it *does* turn out to be a poltergeist," Alsgood said, "if things *do* get a lot worse, will you call me right away? I've been fortunate enough to observe two poltergeists, as I said. I'd like nothing better than to see a third going through its tricks. The opportunity doesn't arise very often."

"I guess not," Paul said.

"So you'll call me?"

"I very much doubt there's a poltergeist involved here, Mr. Alsgood. If I keep looking long enough and hard enough, I'll find a perfectly logical explanation for what's been happening. But on the off-chance that it *is* a malign spirit, rest assured I'll give you a call the moment the first refrigerator or chiffonier levitates."

Alsgood wasn't able to see anything amusing about their conversation. He frowned when he detected levity in Paul's voice, and he said, "I didn't really expect you to take me seriously."

"Oh, please don't think I'm not grateful for—"

"No, no," Alsgood said, waving him to silence. "I understand. No offense taken." The excitement had gone out of his watery eyes. "You've been raised to believe strictly in science. You've been taught to put your faith only in things that can be seen and touched and measured. That's the modern way." His shoulders slumped. The color in his face faded, and his skin became pale, grayish, and slack, as it had been a few minutes ago. "Asking you to be open-minded about ghosts is as pointless as trying to convince a deep-sea creature that there are such things as birds. It's sad but true, and I have no reason to be angry about it." He opened the front door, and the sound of the rain grew louder. "Anyway, for your sake, I hope it isn't a poltergeist you've got here. I hope you find that logical explanation you're looking for. I really do, Mr. Tracy."

Before Paul could respond, Alsgood turned and walked out into the rain. He no longer seemed like a zealot; there was no trace of passion in him. He was just a thin, gray man, shuffling through the gray mist, head slightly bowed against the gray rain, illuminated by the gray light of the storm; he almost seemed like a ghost himself.

Paul closed the door, put his back against it, and looked around the hall, through the nearest archway, which opened onto the living room. Poltergeist? Not very damned likely.

He preferred Alsgood's other suggestion: that the hammering might simply stop as suddenly and inexplicably as it had started, without the cause ever being known.

He glanced at his watch. 6:06.

Carol had said she would remain at the hospital until eight o'clock and would then come home for a late meal. That gave him an hour or so to work on his novel before he had to start cooking dinner— broiled chicken breasts, steamed vegetables, and rice with bits of green pepper.

He went upstairs to his office and sat down at the

typewriter. He picked up the last page he had written, intending to reread it a few times and get back into the mood and tone of the story he was telling.

THUNK! THUNK!

The house shook. The windows rattled.

He bolted up from his chair.

THUNK!

On his desk, the jar full of pens and pencils toppled over, cracked into several pieces, and spilled its contents onto the floor.

Silence.

He waited. One minute. Two minutes.

Nothing.

There was no sound except the snapping of the rain against the windows and the drumming of it on the roof.

Only three hammer blows this time. Harder than any that had come before. But only three. Almost as if someone were playing games with him, taunting him.

●||●||●

Shortly before midnight, in room 316, the girl laughed softly in her sleep.

Outside her window, lightning pulsed, and the night flickered, and the darkness seemed to gallop for a moment, as if it were a huge and eager beast.

The girl turned onto her stomach without waking, murmured into her pillows. "The ax," she said with a wistful sigh. "The ax . . ."

●||●||●

On the stroke of midnight, just forty minutes after she had fallen asleep, Carol bolted up from her pillows, trembling violently. As she struggled out of the grip of her nightmare, she heard someone say, "It's coming! It's coming!" She stared wildly, blindly into the lightless room until she realized the panic-stricken voice had been her own.

Suddenly she could not tolerate the darkness one second longer. She fumbled desperately for the switch on the bedside lamp, found it, and sagged with relief.

The light didn't disturb Paul. He mumbled in his sleep but didn't wake.

Carol leaned back against the headboard and listened to her racing heart as it gradually slowed to a normal beat.

Her hands were icy. She put them under the covers and curled them into warming fists.

The nightmares have got to stop, she told herself. I can't go through this every night. I need my sleep.

Perhaps a vacation was called for. She had been working too hard for too long. The accumulated weariness was probably partly to blame for her bad dreams. She had also been under a great deal of unusual stress lately: the pending adoption, the near-tragic events in O'Brian's office on Wednesday, the accident just yesterday morning, the girl's amnesia for which she felt responsible. . . . Living with too much tension could cause exceptionally vivid nightmares of the sort she was experiencing. A week in the mountains, away from everyday problems, seemed like the perfect medicine.

In addition to all the other sources of stress, *that* day was approaching, the birthday of the child she had put up for adoption. A week from tomorrow, the

Saturday after next, would mark sixteen years since
she had relinquished the baby. Already, eight days
in advance of that anniversary, she was burdened by
a heavy mantle of guilt. By the time next Saturday
rolled around, she would most likely be thoroughly
depressed, as usual. A week in the mountains, away
from everyday problems, might be the perfect medicine for *that* ailment, too.

Last year, she and Paul had purchased a vacation
cabin on an acre of timbered land in the mountains.
It was a cozy place—two bedrooms, one bath, a living
room with a big stone fireplace, and a complete
kitchen—a retreat that combined all the comforts of
civilization with the clean air, marvelous scenery, and
tranquility that could not be found in the city.

They had planned to get away to the cabin at least
two weekends every month during the summer, but
they had made the trip only three times in the past
four months, less than half as often as they had hoped.
Paul had labored hard to meet a series of self-imposed
deadlines on his novel, and she had taken on more
patients—a couple of really troubled kids who simply
could not be turned away—and for both herself and
Paul, work had expanded to fill every spare moment.
Perhaps they were the overachievers that Alfred
O'Brian had thought they might be.

But we'll change when we have a child, Carol told
herself. We'll make lots of time for leisure and for
family outings because creating the best environment
for our child is the job we're looking forward to more
than any other.

Now, sitting up in bed, the grisly nightmare still
chillingly fresh in her mind, she decided to start
changing her life from this moment on. They *would*

take off a few days, maybe a whole week, and go to the mountains before the recommendations committee's meeting at the end of the month, so they would be rested and composed when at last they met the child who would be theirs. They couldn't take off this coming week, of course. She would need time to reschedule her appointments. Besides, she didn't want to leave town until Jane Doe's parents showed up and properly identified the girl; that might take a few more days. But they ought to be able to carve a large chunk of time out of the week after next, and she made up her mind to start nudging Paul about it first thing in the morning.

Having reached that decision, she felt better. The mere prospect of a vacation, even a brief one, relieved much of her tension.

She looked at Paul and said, "I love you."

He continued to snore softly.

Smiling, she clicked off the light and settled under the covers again. For a couple of minutes she listened to the rain and to her husband's rhythmic breathing; then she drifted into a sound, satisfying sleep.

●‖●‖●

Rain fell throughout Saturday, rounding out a monotonously watery, sunless week. The day was cool, too, and the wind had teeth.

Carol visited Jane in the hospital on Saturday afternoon. They played cards and talked about some of the articles the girl had read in the magazines Carol had bought for her. Through every conversation, regardless of the subject, Carol probed continuously but subtly at the girl's amnesia, prodded her memory without letting her see that she was being prodded. But it was all wasted effort, for Jane's past remained beyond her grasp.

At the end of the afternoon visiting hours, as Carol was heading toward the elevators on the third floor, she encountered Dr. Sam Hannaport in the corridor.

"Haven't the police come up with any leads at all?" she asked.

He shrugged his burly shoulders. "Not yet."

"It's been over two days since the accident."

"Which isn't all that long."

"It seems like an eternity to that poor kid in there," Carol said, gesturing toward the door of 316.

"I know," Hannaport said. "And I feel just as bad about it as you do. But it's still too soon to be pessimistic."

"If *I* had a girl like her, and if *my* kid turned up missing for even one day, I'd be pushing the police hard, and I'd make damned sure the story was in all the papers, and I'd be pounding on doors and making a nuisance of myself all over the city."

Hannaport nodded. "I know you would. I've seen how you operate, and I admire your style. And listen, I think your visits with the girl have an awful lot to do with keeping her spirits up. It's good of you to take all this time with her."

"Well, I'm not angling for a testimonial dinner," Carol said. "I don't think I'm doing any more than I have to do. I mean, I've got a responsibility here."

A nurse came along, pushing a patient in a wheelchair. Carol and Hannaport stepped out of the way.

"At least Jane seems to be in good physical shape," Carol said.

"Like I told you on Wednesday—there were no

serious injuries. In fact, because she *is* in such good condition, she presents us with a problem. She doesn't really belong in a hospital. I just hope her parents show up before I'm forced to discharge her."

"Discharge her? But you can't do that if she has nowhere to go. She can't cope outside. For God's sake, she doesn't even know who she is!"

"Naturally, I'll keep her here as long as I possibly can. But by late tonight or tomorrow morning, all of our beds are probably going to be full. Then, if the number of emergency admissions is greater than the number of discharges already scheduled, we'll have to look around for a few other patients who can be safely released. Jane's bound to be one of them. If some guy's brought in here with a cracked skull from an auto accident, or if an ambulance delivers a woman who's been stabbed by a jealous boyfriend, I can't justify turning away seriously injured people while I'm keeping a perfectly healthy girl whose worst physical problem is a contusion on her left shoulder."

"But her amnesia—"

"Is something we can't treat anyway."

"But she has nowhere to go," Carol said. "What would happen to her?"

In his calm, soft, reassuring voice, Hannaport said, "She'll be okay. Really. We're not going to just abandon her. We'll petition to have her declared a ward of the court until her parents show up. In the meantime, she'll do just as well at some minimal-care facility as she would do here."

"What facility are you talking about?"

"Just three blocks from here, there's a home for runaway and pregnant teenage girls, and it's far cleaner and better managed than the average state institution."

"The Polmar Home," Carol said. "I know it."

"Then you know it's not a dungeon or a dump."

"I still don't like moving her out of here," Carol said. "She's going to feel as if she's being shunted aside, forgotten, and left to rot. She's on very shaky ground already. This'll scare her half to death."

Frowning, Hannaport said, "I don't like it much myself, but I truly don't have an option. If we're short on bed space, the law says we've got to consider degrees of need and take in those patients who have the most to lose by being denied care or by having treatment delayed. I'm in a bind."

"I understand. I'm not blaming you. Dammit, if someone would just come forward to claim her!"

"Someone might, any minute."

Carol shook her head. "No. I've got a feeling it's not going to be that easy. Have you told Jane yet?"

"No. We won't make the petition to the court sooner than Monday morning, so I might as well wait until tomorrow to explain it to her. Maybe something'll happen between now and then to make it unnecessary. No use worrying her until we have to."

Carol was depressed, remembering her own days in a state-run institution, before Grace had come along to rescue her. She had been a tough kid, street-smart, but the experience had nevertheless scarred her. Jane was bright and spunky and strong and sweet, but she wasn't *tough*, not like Carol had been at her age. What would institutional living do to her if she had to endure it for more than a day or two? If she was simply dropped in among kids who *were* street-smart, among kids who had drug and behavioral problems, she would most likely be victimized, perhaps even violently. What she needed was a real home, love, guidance—

"Of course!" Carol said. She grinned.

Hannaport looked at her questioningly.

"Why can't she come with *me*?" Carol asked.

"What?"

"Look, Dr. Hannaport, if it's all right with Paul, my husband, why couldn't you recommend to the court that I be awarded temporary custody of Jane until someone shows up who can identify her?"

"You really better think twice about that," Hannaport said. "Taking her in, disrupting your lives—"

"It won't be a disruption," Carol said. "It'll be a pleasure. She's a delightful kid."

Hannaport stared at her a long moment, searching her face and her eyes.

"After all," Carol argued as persuasively as she could, "the only kind of doctor who might be able to cure Jane's amnesia is a psychiatrist. And in case you've forgotten, that's what I am. I'd not only be able to provide a decent home for her; I'd also be able to treat her rather intensively."

Finally, Hannaport smiled. "I think it's a grand and generous offer, Dr. Tracy."

"Then you'll make the recommendation to the court?"

"Yes. Of course, you never can be sure what a judge will do. But I think there's a pretty good chance he'll see where the best interests of the girl lie."

●H●H●

A few minutes later, in the hospital lobby, Carol used a pay phone to call Paul. She recounted the conversation she'd had with Dr. Hannaport, but before she got to the big question, Paul interrupted her. "You want to make a place for Jane," he said.

Surprised, Carol said, "How'd you guess?"

He laughed. "I know you, sugarface. When it comes to kids, you've got a heart the consistency of vanilla pudding."

"She won't be in your way," Carol said quickly. "She won't distract you from your writing. And now that O'Brian won't be able to present our application for the adoption until the end of the month, there's no chance we'll have *two* kids to take care of. In fact maybe the delay at the agency was meant to be—so we'd have a place for Jane until her folks show up. It's only temporary, Paul. Really. And we—"

"Okay, okay," he said. "You don't have to sell me on it. I approve of the plan."

"If you'd like to come here and meet Jane first, that's—"

"No, no. I'm sure she's everything you've said she is. Don't forget, though, you were planning to go to the mountains in a week or so."

"We might not even have Jane that long. And if we do, we can probably take her with us, so long as we let the court know where we're going."

"When do we have to appear in court?"

"I don't know. Probably Monday or Tuesday."

"I'll be on my best behavior," Paul said.

"Scrub behind your ears?"

"Okay. And I'll also wear shoes."

Grinning, Carol said, "Don't pick your nose in front of the judge."

"Not unless he picks his first."

She said, "I love you, Dr. Tracy."

"I love *you*, Dr. Tracy."

When she put down the receiver and turned away from the pay phone, she felt wonderful. Not even the gaudy decor of the visitors' lounge could get on her nerves now.

●‖●‖●

That night, there was no hammering sound in the Tracy house, no evidence of the poltergeist that Mr. Alsgood had warned Paul about. There was no disturbance the following day, either, and none the day after that. The strange noise and the vibrations had ceased as inexplicably as they had begun.

Carol stopped having nightmares, too. She slept deeply, peacefully, without interruption. She quickly forgot about the flickering, silvery blade of the ax swinging back and forth in the strange void.

The weather improved, too. The clouds dissipated on Sunday. Monday was summery, blue.

●‖●‖●

Tuesday afternoon, while Paul and Carol were in court trying to obtain temporary custody of Jane Doe, Grace Mitowski was cleaning her kitchen. She had just finished dusting the top of the refrigerator when the telephone rang.

"Hello."

No one answered her.

"Hello," she said again.

A thin, whispery, male voice said, "Grace..."

"Yes?"

His words were muffled, and there was an echo on the line, as if he were talking into a tin can.

"I can't understand you," she said. "Can you speak up?"

He tried, but again the words were lost. They seemed to be coming from an enormous distance, across an unimaginably vast chasm.

"We have a terrible connection," she said. "You'll have to speak up."

"Grace," he said, his voice only slightly louder. "Gracie...it's almost too late. You've got to ...move fast. You've got to stop it... from happening ...again." It was a dry, brittle voice; it cracked repeatedly, with a sound like dead autumn leaves underfoot. "It's almost...too late...too late...."

She recognized the voice, and she froze. Her hand tightened on the receiver, and she couldn't get her breath.

"Gracie...it can't go on forever. You've got ...to put an end to it. Protect her, Gracie. Protect her...."

The voice faded away.

There was only silence. But not the silence of an open phone line. There was no hissing. No electronic beeping in the background. This was perfect silence, utterly unmarred by even the slightest click or whistle of electronic circuitry. Vast silence. Endless.

She put the phone down.

She started to shake.

She went to the cupboard and got down the bottle of Scotch she kept for visitors. She poured herself a double shot and sat down at the kitchen table.

The liquor didn't warm her. Chills still shook her.

The voice on the phone had belonged to Leonard. Her husband. He had been dead for eighteen years.

PART TWO

Evil Walks Among Us...

Evil is no faceless stranger,
living in a distant neighborhood.
Evil has a wholesome, hometown face,
with merry eyes and an open smile.
Evil walks among us, wearing a mask
which looks like all our faces.

—*The Book of Counted Sorrows*

7

TUESDAY, after winning temporary custody of Jane Doe, Paul went home to work on his novel, and Carol took the girl shopping. Because Jane had no clothes except those she'd been wearing when she'd stepped in front of the Volkswagen last Thursday morning, she needed a lot of things, even for just a few days. She was embarrassed about spending Carol's money, and at first she was reluctant to admit that she liked anything she saw or that anything fit her well enough to buy it.

At last Carol said, "Honey, you *need* this stuff, so please just relax and let me buy it for you. Okay? In the long run, it won't be coming out of my pocket anyway. I'll most likely be reimbursed either by your parents, by the foster children program, or by some other county agency."

That argument worked. They quickly purchased a couple of pairs of jeans, a few blouses, underwear, a good pair of sneakers, socks, a sweater, and a windbreaker.

When they got home, Jane was impressed by the Tudor house with its leaded-glass windows, gabled roof, and stonework. She fell in love with the guest room in which she was to stay. It had a cove ceiling, a long window seat inset in a bay window, and a wall of mirrored closet doors. It was done in deep blue and pale beige, with Queen Anne furniture of lustrous cherrywood. "It's really just a guest room?" Jane asked, incredulous. "You don't use it regularly? Boy, if this were my house, I'd come in here all the time! I'd just sit and read for a little while every day—read and sit there in the window and soak up the atmosphere."

Carol had always liked the room, but through Jane's eyes she achieved a new perception and appreciation of it. As she watched the girl inspecting things—sliding open the closet doors, checking the view from each angle of the bay window, testing the firmness of the mattress on the queen-sized bed— Carol realized that one advantage of having children was that their innocent, fresh reactions to everything could keep their parents young and open-minded, too.

That evening, Carol, Paul, and Jane prepared dinner together. The girl fit in comfortably and immediately, in spite of the fact that she was somewhat shy. There was a lot of laughter in the kitchen and at the dinner table.

After dinner, Jane started washing dishes while Carol and Paul cleared the table. When they were separated from the girl for a moment, alone in the dining room, Paul said quietly, "She's a terrific kid."

"Didn't I tell you so?"

"Funny thing, though."

"What?"

"Ever since I saw her this afternoon, outside the courtroom," Paul said, "I've had the feeling that I've seen her somewhere before."

"Where?"

He shook his head. "I'll be damned if I know. But there's something familiar about her face."

⊚‖⊛‖⊚

Throughout Tuesday afternoon, Grace expected the phone to ring again.

She dreaded having to answer it.

She tried to work off her nervous energy by cleaning the house. She scrubbed the kitchen floor, dusted the furniture in every room, and swept all the carpets.

But she couldn't stop thinking about the call: the paper-dry, echo-distorted voice that had sounded like Leonard; the odd things he had said; the eerie silence when he had finished speaking; the disquieting sense of vast distances, an unimaginable gulf of space and time. . . .

It had to be a hoax. But who could be responsible for it? And why torment her with an imitation of Leonard's voice, eighteen years after the man had died? What was the point of playing games like this *now*, after so much time had passed?

She tried to get her mind off the call by baking apple dumplings. Thick, crusty dumplings—served with cinnamon, milk, and just a bit of sugar—were a suppertime favorite of hers, for she had been born and raised in Lancaster, the heart of the Pennsylvania Dutch country, where that dish was considered a meal in itself. But Tuesday evening, she had no appetite, not even for dumplings. She ate a few bites, but she couldn't even finish half of one dumpling, though she usually ate two whole ones in a single meal.

She was still picking disinterestedly at her food when the telephone rang.

Her head jerked up. She stared at the wall phone that was above the small, built-in desk beside the refrigerator.

It rang again. And again.

Trembling, she got up, went to the phone, and lifted the receiver.

"Gracie..."

The voice was faint but intelligible.

"Gracie... it's almost too late."

It was him. Leonard. Or someone who sounded exactly like Leonard had sounded.

She couldn't respond to him. Her throat clutched tight.

"Gracie..."

Her legs seemed to be melting under her. She pulled out the chair that was tucked into the kneehole of the desk, and she sat down quickly.

"Gracie... stop it from happening again. It mustn't... go on forever... time after time... the blood... the murder...."

She closed her eyes, forced herself to speak. Her voice was weak, quavery. She didn't even recognize it as her own. It was the voice of a stranger—a weary, frightened, frail old woman. "Who is this?"

The whispery, vibrative voice on the telephone said, "Protect her, Gracie."

"What do you want from me?"

"Protect her."

"Why are you doing this?"

"Protect her."

"Protect who?" she demanded.

"Willa. Protect Willa."

She was still frightened and confused, but she was beginning to be angry, too. "I don't *know* anyone named Willa, dammit! Who is this?"

"Leonard."

"No! Do you think I'm a doddering, senile old fool? Leonard's dead. Eighteen years! You're not Leonard. What kind of game are you playing?"

She wanted to hang up on him, and she knew that was the best thing to do with a crank like this, but she couldn't make herself put down the receiver. He sounded so much like Leonard that she was mesmerized by his voice.

He spoke again, much softer than before, but she could still hear him. "Protect Willa."

"I tell you, I don't know her. And if you keep calling me with this nonsense, I'm going to tell the police that some sick practical joker is—"

"Carol . . . Carol," the man said, his voice fading syllable by syllable. "Willa . . . but you call her . . . Carol."

"What the hell is going on here?"

"Beware . . . the . . . cat."

"What?"

The voice was so distant now that she had to strain to hear it. "The . . . cat . . ."

"Aristophanes? What about him? Have you done something to him? Have you poisoned him? Is that what's been wrong with him lately?"

No response.

"Are you there?"

Nothing.

"What about the cat?" she demanded.

No answer.

She listened to the pure, pure silence, and she began to tremble so violently that she had trouble holding the phone. "Who are you? Why do you want to torment me like this? Why do you want to hurt Aristophanes?"

Far, far away, the achingly familiar voice of her long-dead husband uttered a few final, barely audible words. "Wish...I was there...for the...apple dumplings."

●‖◉‖◉●

They had forgotten to buy pajamas for Jane. She went to bed in knee socks, panties, and one of Carol's T-shirts, which was a bit large for her.

"What happens tomorrow?" she asked when she was tucked in, her head raised on a plump pillow.

Carol sat on the edge of the bed. "I thought we might start a program of treatment designed to pry open your memory."

"What kind of treatment?"

"Do you know what hypnotic regression therapy is?"

Jane was suddenly frightened. Several times since the accident, she had made a conscious, concerted effort to remember who she was, but on each occasion, as she felt herself coming close to a disturbing revelation, she had become dizzy, disoriented, and panicky. When she pressed her mind back, back, back toward the truth, a psychological defense mechanism cut off her curiosity as abruptly as a strangler's garrotte might have cut off her air supply. And every time, on the edge of unconsciousness, she saw a strange, silvery object swinging back and forth through blackness, an utterly indecipherable yet blood-chilling vision. She sensed there was something hideous in her past, something so terrible that she would be better off *not* remembering. She had just about made up her mind not to seek what had been lost, to accept her new life as a nameless orphan, even though it might be filled with hardships. But through hypnotic regression therapy, she could be forced to confront the specter in her past, whether she wanted to or not. That prospect filled her with dread.

"Are you all right?" Carol asked.

The girl blinked, licked her lips. "Yeah. I was just thinking about what you said. Hypnotic regression. Does that mean you're going to put me in a trance and make me remember everything?"

"Well, it isn't that easy, honey. There's no guarantee it'll work. I'll hypnotize you and ask you to think back to the accident on Thursday morning; then I'll nudge you further and further into the past. If you're a good subject, you might remember who you are and where you come from. Hypnotic regression is a tool that comes in handy sometimes when I'm trying to get a patient to relive a deeply hidden, severely regressed trauma. I've never used the technique on an amnesia victim, but I know it's applicable to a case like yours. Of course, it only works about half the time. And when it does work, it takes more than one or two sessions. It can be a tedious, frustrating process. We're not going to get much of anywhere

tomorrow, and in fact your parents will probably show
up before I've been able to help you remember. But
we might as well make a start. That is, if it's all right
with you."

She didn't want Carol to know that she was afraid
to remember, so she said, "Oh, sure! It sounds fascinating."

"I've got four patients scheduled for tomorrow, but
I can work you in at eleven o'clock. You'll have to
spend a lot of time in the waiting room, before and
after your session, so first thing in the morning, we'll
find a book for you to take along. Do you like to read
mystery stories?"

"I guess so."

"Agatha Christie?"

"The name's familiar, but I don't know whether
I've ever read any of her books."

"You can try one tomorrow. If you were a big fan
of mysteries, maybe Agatha Christie will open your
memory for you. Any stimulus, any connection whatsoever with your past can act like a doorway." She
leaned down, kissed Jane's forehead. "But don't
worry about it now. Just get a good night's sleep,
kiddo."

After Carol left the room, closing the door behind
her, Jane didn't immediately switch off the light. She
let her gaze travel slowly around the room and then
slowly back again, her eyes resting on each point of
beauty.

Please, God, she thought, let me stay here. Somehow, some way, let me stay in this house forever and
ever. Don't make me go back where I came from,
wherever that might be. This is where I want to live.
This is where I want to *die*, it's so pretty.

Finally, she reached out and snapped off the bed-side lamp.

Darkness folded in like bat wings.

●II●II●

Using a piece of Masonite and four nails, Grace Mitowski fixed a temporary seal over the inside of the pet door.

Aristophanes stood in the center of the kitchen, his head cocked to one side, watching her with bright-eyed interest. Every few seconds, he meowed in what seemed to be an inquisitive tone.

When the last nail was in place, Grace said, "Okay, cat. For the time being, your license to roam has been suspended. There might be a man out there who's been feeding you small amounts of drugs or poison of some sort, and maybe that's been the cause of your bad behavior. We'll just have to wait and see if you improve. Have you been flying high on drugs, you silly cat?"

Aristophanes meowed questioningly.

"Yes," Grace said. "I know it sounds bizarre. But if it's not some kook I've got to deal with, then it really must've been Leonard on the phone. And that's even *more* bizarre, don't you think?"

The cat turned his head from one side to the other, as if he really were trying to make sense of what she was saying.

Grace stopped, held out her hand, and rubbed her thumb and forefinger together. "Here, kitty. Here, kitty-kitty-kitty."

Aristophanes hissed, spat, turned, and ran.

●II●II●

For a change, they made love with the lights off.
Carol's breath was hot against his neck. She pressed
close, rocked and tensed and twisted and flexed in
perfect harmony with him; her exquisite, pneumatic
movements were as fluid as currents in a warm river.
She arched her elegant back, lifted and subsided in
tempo with his measured strokes. She was as pliant,
as silken, and eventually as all-encompassing as the
darkness.

Afterwards, they held hands and talked about in-
consequential things, steadily growing drowsy. Carol
fell asleep while Paul was talking. When she failed
to respond to one of his questions, he gently disen-
tangled his hand from hers.

He was tired, but he couldn't find sleep as quickly
as she had found it. He kept thinking about the girl.
He was certain he had seen her prior to their meeting
outside the courtroom this morning. During dinner,
her face had grown more and more familiar. It continued to haunt him. But no matter how hard he tried,
he couldn't recall where else he had seen her.

As he lay in the dark bedroom, paging through his
memory, he gradually became uneasy. He began to
feel—utterly without reason—that his previous en-
counter with Jane had been strange, perhaps even
unpleasant. Then he wondered if the girl might actually pose some sort of threat to Carol and himself.

But that's absurd, he thought. Doesn't make any
sense at all. I must be even more tired than I thought.
Logic seems to be slipping out of my grasp. What
possible threat could Jane pose? She's such a nice

kid. An exceptionally nice kid.

He sighed, rolled over, and thought about the plot of his first novel (the failed one), and that quickly put him to sleep.

●II●II●

At one o'clock in the morning, Grace Mitowski was sitting up in bed, watching a late movie on the Sony portable. She was vaguely aware that Humphrey Bogart and Lauren Bacall were engaged in witty repartee, but she didn't really hear anything they said. She had lost track of the film's plot only minutes after she had turned it on.

She was thinking about Leonard, the husband she had lost to cancer eighteen years ago. He had been a good man, hard-working, generous, loving, a grand conversationalist. She had loved him very much.

But not *everyone* had loved Leonard. He had had his faults, of course. The worst thing about him had been his impatience—and the sharp tongue that his impatience had encouraged. He couldn't tolerate people who were lazy or apathetic or ignorant or foolish. "Which includes two-thirds of the human race," he had often said when he was feeling especially curmudgeonly. Because he was an honest man with precious little diplomacy in his bones, he had told people exactly what he thought of them. As a result, he had led a life remarkably free of deception but rich in enemies.

She wondered if it had been one of those enemies who had called her, pretending to be Leonard. A sick man might get as much pleasure from tormenting

Leonard's widow as he would have gotten from tormenting Leonard himself. He might get a thrill from poisoning her cat and from harassing her with weird phone calls.

But after *eighteen years*? Who would have remembered Leonard's voice so well as to be able to imitate it perfectly such a long time later? Surely she was the only person in the world who could still recognize that voice upon hearing it speak only a word or two. And why bring Carol into it? Leonard had died three years before Carol had entered Grace's life; he had never known the girl. His enemies couldn't possibly have anything against Carol. What had the caller meant when he'd referred to Carol as "Willa"? And, most disturbing of all, how did the caller know she had just made apple dumplings?

There *was* another explanation, though she was loath to consider it. Perhaps the caller hadn't been an old enemy of Leonard's. Maybe the call actually had come from Leonard himself. From a dead man.

—*No. Impossible.*

—*A lot of people believe in ghosts.*

—*Not me.*

She thought about the strange dreams she'd had last week. She hadn't believed in dream prophecies then. Now she did. So why not ghosts, too?

No. She was a level-headed woman who had lived a stable, rational life, who had been trained in the sciences, who had always believed that science held all the answers. Now, at seventy years of age, if she made room for the existence of ghosts within her otherwise rational philosophy, she might be opening the floodgates on madness. If you truly believed in ghosts, what came next? Vampires? Did you have to start carrying a sharp wooden stake and a crucifix everywhere you went? Werewolves? Better buy a box of silver bullets! Evil elves who lived in the center of the earth and caused quakes and volcanoes? Sure! Why not?

Grace laughed bitterly.

She couldn't suddenly become a believer in ghosts, because acceptance of that superstition might require the acceptance of countless others. She was too old, too comfortable with herself, too accustomed to her familiar ways to reconsider her entire view of life. And she certainly wasn't going to contemplate such a sweeping reevaluation merely because she had received two bizarre phone calls.

That left only one thing to be decided: whether or not she should tell Carol that someone was harassing her and had used Carol's name. She tried to hear how she would sound when she explained the telephone calls and when she outlined her theory about Aristophanes being drugged or poisoned. She couldn't hope to sound like the Grace Mitowski that everyone knew. She'd come off like an hysterical old woman who was seeing nonexistent conspirators behind every door and under every bed.

They might even think she was going senile.

Am I? she wondered. Did I imagine the telephone calls? No. Surely not.

She wasn't imagining Aristophanes's changed personality, either. She looked at the claw marks on the palm of her hand; although they were healing, they were still red and puffy. Proof. Those marks were proof that *something* was wrong.

I'm not senile, she told herself. Not even a little bit. But I sure don't want to have to convince Carol or Paul that I've got all my marbles, once I've told them that I'm getting phone calls from Leonard. Better go easy for the time being. Wait. See what happens next. Anyway, I can figure this out on my own. I can handle it.

On the Sony, Bogart and Bacall grinned at each other.

●ıı●ıı●

When Jane woke up in the middle of the night, she discovered she had been sleepwalking. She was in the kitchen, but she couldn't recall getting out of bed and coming downstairs.

The kitchen was silent. The only sound was from the softly purring refrigerator. The only light was from the moon, but because the moon was full and because the kitchen had quite a few windows, there was enough light to see by.

Jane was standing at a counter near the sink. She had opened one of the drawers and had taken a butcher knife out of it.

She stared down at the knife, startled to find it in her hand.

Pale moonlight glinted on the cold blade.

She returned the knife to the drawer.

Closed the drawer.

She had been gripping the knife so tightly that her hand ached.

Why did I want a knife?

A chill skittered like a centipede along her spine.

Her bare arms and legs broke out in gooseflesh, and she was suddenly very aware that she was wearing only a T-shirt, panties, and knee socks.

The refrigerator motor shut off with a dry rattle that made her jump and turn.

Now the house was preternaturally silent. She could almost believe that she had gone deaf.

What was I doing with the knife?

She hugged herself to ward off the chills that kept wriggling through her.

Maybe she had dreamed about food and had come down here in her sleep to make a sandwich. Yes. That was probably what had happened. In fact she *was* a bit hungry. So she had gotten the knife out of the drawer in order to slice some roast beef for a sandwich. There was a butt end of a roast in the refrigerator. She had seen it earlier, when she had been helping Carol and Paul make dinner.

But now she didn't think she could eat a sandwich or anything else. Her bare legs were getting colder by the moment, and she felt immodestly exposed in just flimsy panties and a thin T-shirt. All she wanted now was to get back to bed, under the covers.

Climbing the steps in the darkness, she stayed close to the wall, where the treads were less likely to creak. She returned to her room without waking anyone.

Outside, a dog howled in the distance.

Jane burrowed deeper in her blankets.

For a while she had trouble getting to sleep because she felt guilty about prowling through the house while the Tracys slept. She felt sneaky. She felt as if she had been taking advantage of their hospitality.

Of course, that was silly. She hadn't been nosing around on purpose. She had been sleepwalking, and there was no way a person could control something like that.

Just sleepwalking.

8

THE focal point of Carol Tracy's office was Mickey Mouse. One long wall of the room was fitted with shelves on which were displayed Mickey Mouse memorabilia. There were Mickey Mouse buttons, Mickey Mouse pins, a wristwatch, belt buckles, a Mickey Mouse phone, drinking glasses bearing the famous mouse's countenance, a beer mug on which there was a likeness of Mickey dressed in lederhosen and a Tyrolean hat. But mostly there were statuettes of the cartoon star: Mickey standing beside a little red car; Mickey curled up in striped pajamas. sleeping; Mickey dancing a jig; Mickey with Minnie; Mickey with Goofy; Mickey holding barbells; Mickey with Pluto; Mickey and Donald Duck with their arms around each other's shoulders, looking like the best of friends; Mickey riding a horse, with a cowboy hat raised in one white-gloved, four-fingered hand; Mickey dressed like a soldier, a sailor, a doctor; Mickey in swimming trunks, clutching a surfboard. There were wooden, metal, chalk, porcelain, plastic, glass, and clay statuettes of Mickey; some of them were a foot high, and some were no more than one inch tall, though most were in between. The only thing those hundreds of Mickeys had in common was the fact that every one of them was smiling broadly.

The collection was an icebreaker with patients of all ages. No one could resist Mickey Mouse.

Jane responded as scores of patients had done before her. She said "oooh" and "aaah" a lot, and she laughed happily. By the time she had finished admiring the collection and had sat down in one of the big leather armchairs, she was ready for the therapy session; her tension and apprehension had disappeared. Mickey had worked his usual magic.

Carol didn't have an analyst's couch in her office. She preferred to conduct sessions from a large wing chair, with the patient seated in an identical chair on the other side of the octagonal coffee table. The drapes were always kept tightly shut; soft, golden light was provided by shaded floor lamps. Except for the wall of Mickey Mouse images, the room had a nineteenth-century air.

They chatted about the collection for a couple of minutes, and then Carol said, "Okay, honey. I think we ought to begin."

Worry lines appeared on the girl's forehead. "You really think this hypnosis is a good idea?"

"Yes. I think it's the best tool we have for restoring your memory. Don't worry. It's a simple process. Just relax and flow with it. Okay?"

"Well . . . okay."

Carol got up and stepped around the coffee table, and Jane started to get up, too. "No, you stay there," Carol said. She moved behind the wing chair and put her fingertips against the girl's temples. "Relax, honey. Lean back. Hands in your lap. Palms up, fingers slack. That's fine. Now close your eyes. Are they closed?"

"Yes."

"Good. Very good. Now I want you to think of a kite. A large, diamond-shaped kite. Picture it in your mind. It's an enormous, blue kite sailing high in the blue sky. Can you see it?"

After a brief hesitation, the girl said, "Yes."

"Watch the kite, honey. See how gently it rises and falls on the currents of air. Rises, falls, up and down, up and down, side to side, sailing so gracefully, far above the earth, halfway between the earth and the clouds, far above your head," Carol said in a mellow, soothing, rhythmic voice as she stared down at the girl's thick blond hair. "While you're watching the kite, you'll gradually become as light and as free as it is. You'll learn to soar up and up into the blue sky, just like the kite." With her fingertips, she lightly traced circles on the girl's temples. "All the tension is leaving you, all the worries and cares are floating away, away, until the only thought in your head is the kite, the sailing kite in the blue sky. A great weight has been removed from your skull, from your forehead and your temples. Already, you feel much lighter." She moved her hands down to the girl's neck. "The muscles in your neck are relaxing. Tension is dropping away. A great weight is dropping away. You are so much lighter now that you can almost feel yourself

rising up toward the kite...almost...almost..."
She moved her hands down, touched the girl's shoulders. "Relax. Let the tension fall away. Like blocks of concrete. Making you lighter, lighter. A weight is falling off your chest, too. And now you're floating. Just a few inches off the ground, but you *are* floating."

"Yes...floating..." she said, her voice thick.

"The kite is gliding far above, but you are slowly, slowly moving up to join it...."

She went on like that for a minute, then returned to her own chair and sat down.

Jane was slumped in the other wing chair, head tilted to one side, eyes closed, face soft and slack, breathing softly.

"You are in a very deep sleep," Carol told her. "A very relaxed, very deep, deep sleep. Do you understand?"

"Yes," the girl murmured.

"You will answer a few questions for me."

"Okay."

"You will remain in your deep sleep, and you will answer my questions until I tell you it's time to wake up. Understood?"

"Yes."

"Good. Very good. Now tell me—what is your name?"

The girl was silent.

"What is your name, honey?"

"Jane."

"Is that your real name?"

"No."

"What is your real name?"

Jane frowned. "I...don't remember."

"Where did you come from?"

"The hospital."

"Before that?"

"Nowhere."

A bead of saliva glistened at the corner of the girl's mouth. Languorously, she licked it away before it could drool down her chin.

Carol said, "Honey, do you remember the Mickey Mouse watch you saw a few minutes ago?"

"Yes."

"Well, I've taken that watch from the shelf," Carol said, though she hadn't moved from her chair. "And now I'm turning the hands on it backwards, around and around the dial, always backwards. Can you see the hands moving backwards on that Mickey Mouse watch?"

"Yes."

"Now something amazing is happening. As I turn those hands backwards and backwards, time itself begins to flow in reverse. It isn't a quarter past eleven any more. It's now eleven o'clock. This is a magic watch. It governs the flow of time. And now it's ten o'clock in the morning...nine o'clock...eight o'clock.... Look around you. Where are you now?"

The girl opened her eyes. They were fixed on a distant point. She said, "Ummm...the kitchen. Yeah. The breakfast nook. Boy, the bacon's nice and crisp."

Gradually, Carol moved her back in time, back through the days she had spent in the hospital, finally regressing to the accident last Thursday morning. The girl winced as she relived the moment of impact, and cried out, and Carol soothed her, and then they went back a few minutes further.

"You're standing on the sidewalk," Carol said.

"You're dressed only in a blouse and jeans. It's raining. Chilly."

The girl closed her eyes again. She shivered.

"What's your name?" Carol asked.

Silence.

"What's your name, honey?"

"I don't know."

"Where have you just come from?"

"Nowhere."

"You mean you have amnesia?"

"Yes."

"Even before the accident?"

"Yes."

Although she was still very concerned about the girl, Carol was relieved to hear that she wasn't responsible for Jane's condition. For a moment she felt like that blue kite, capable of soaring up and away. Then she said, "Okay. You're about to step into the street. Do you just want to cross it, or do you intend to walk in front of a car?"

"I . . . don't . . . know."

"How do you feel? Happy? Depressed? Indifferent?"

"Scared," the girl said in a small, shaky voice.

"What are you scared of?"

Silence.

"What are you scared of?"

"It's coming."

"What's coming?"

"Behind me!"

"What's behind you?"

The girl opened her eyes again. She was still staring at a distant point, but now there was stark terror in her eyes.

"What's behind you?" Carol asked again.

"Oh God," the girl said miserably.

"What is it?"

"No, no." She shook her head. Her face was blood-less.

Carol leaned forward in her chair. "Relax, honey. You will relax and be calm. Close your eyes. Calm... like the kite... far above everything... floating... warm."

The tension went out of Jane's face.

."All right," Carol said. "Staying calm, always relaxed and calm, you will tell me what you're afraid of."

The girl said nothing.

"Honey, what are you scared of? What's behind you?"

"Something..."

"What?"

"Something..."

Patiently, Carol said, "Be specific."

"I... don't know what it is... but it's coming... and it scares me."

"Okay. Let's go back a bit further." Using the image of the backwards-moving hands on the Mickey Mouse wristwatch, she regressed the girl another full day into the past. "Now look around. Where are you?"

"Nowhere."

"What do you see?"

"Nothing."

"You must see something, honey."

"Darkness."

"Are you in a dark room?"

"No."

"Are there walls in the darkness?"

"No."

"Are you outdoors at night?"

"No."

She regressed the girl another day. "Now what do you see?"

"Just the darkness."

"There must be something else."

"No."

"Open your eyes, honey."

The girl obeyed. Her blue eyes were vacant, glassy. "Nothing."

Carol frowned. "Are you sitting or standing in that dark place?"

"I don't know."

"What do you feel under you? A chair? A floor? A bed?"

"Nothing."

"Reach down. Touch the floor."

"There isn't a floor."

Uneasy about the direction the session was taking, Carol shifted in her chair and stared at the girl for a while, wondering what to try next.

After a few seconds, Jane's eyes fluttered and went shut.

Finally, Carol said, "All right. I'm turning the hands of the watch counterclockwise again. Time is flowing in reverse. It will continue to flow backwards, hour by hour, day by day, faster and faster, until you stop me. I want you to stop me only when you come out of the darkness and can tell me where you are. I'm turning the hands now. Backwards... backwards..."

Ten seconds passed in silence. Twenty. Thirty.

After a full minute, Carol said, "Where are you?"

"Nowhere yet."

"Keep going. Backwards... back in time..."

After another minute, Carol began to think something was wrong. She had the disquieting feeling that she was losing control of the situation and placing her patient in some kind of danger that could not be foreseen. But as she was about to call a halt to the regression and bring the girl forward again, Jane spoke at last.

The girl shot up out of the chair, onto her feet, flailing and screaming. "Somebody help me! Mama! Aunt Rachael! For God's sake, help me!"

The voice wasn't Jane's. It came from her mouth, through her tongue and lips, but it didn't sound at all like her. It wasn't merely distorted by panic. It was an entirely different voice from Jane's. It had its own character, its own accent and tone.

"I'm going to die here! Help! *Get me out of here!*"

Carol was on her feet, too. "Honey, stop it. Calm down."

"I'm on fire! I'm on fire!" the girl screamed, and she slapped at her clothes as if trying to put out the flames.

"No!" Carol said sharply. She stepped around the coffee table and managed to seize the girl's arm, taking several glancing blows in the process.

Jane thrashed, tried to break loose.

Carol held on and began to talk softly but insistently to her, calming her down.

Jane stopped struggling, but she began to gasp and wheeze. "Smoke," she said, gagging. "So much smoke."

Carol talked her out of that, too, and gradually brought her down from the peak of hysteria.

At last Jane sank back into the wing chair. She was wan, and her forehead was strung with beads of sweat. Her blue eyes, staring into a distant place and time, looked haunted.

Carol knelt beside the chair and held the girl's hand. "Honey, can you hear me?"

"Yes."

"Are you okay?"

"I'm afraid. . . ."

"There is no fire."

"There was. Everywhere," the girl said, still speaking with the unfamiliar voice.

"There isn't any more. No fire anywhere."

"If you say so."

"I do. I say so. Now tell me your name."

"Laura."

"Do you remember your last name?"

"Laura Havenswood."

Carol flushed with triumph. "Very good. That's just fine. Where's your home, Laura?"

"Shippensburg."

Shippensburg was a small town less than an hour from Harrisburg. It was a quiet, pleasant place that existed to serve a flourishing state college and a large number of surrounding farms.

"Do you know the address where you live in Shippensburg?" Carol asked.

"There's no street name. It's a farm. Just outside of town, off Walnut Bottom Road."

"So you could take me there if you had to?"

"Oh, yes. It's a pretty place. There are a pair of stone gateposts by the verge of the county lane; they mark the entrance to our land. And there's a long drive flanked by maples, and there are big oaks around the house. It's cool and breezy in the summer with all those shade trees."

"What's your father's first name?"

"Nicholas."

"And his phone number?"

The girl frowned. "His what?"

"What's the telephone number at your house?"

The girl shook her head. "I don't know what you mean."

"Don't you have a telephone?"

"What *is* a telephone?" the girl asked.

Carol stared at her, puzzled. It wasn't possible for a person under hypnosis to be coy or to make jokes of this sort. As she considered her next move, she saw that Laura was becoming agitated again. The girl's brow furrowed, and her eyes widened. She started breathing hard again.

"Laura, listen to me. You will be calm. You will relax and—"

The girl writhed uncontrollably in her chair. Squealing and gasping, she slid off the chair, rolled onto the floor, bumping the coffee table and pushing it aside. She twisted and shuddered and wriggled as if she were having a severe epileptic fit, though she was not; she brushed frantically at herself, for again she seemed to believe she was on fire. She called for someone named Rachael and choked on nonexistent smoke.

Carol required almost a minute to talk her down, which was a serious loss of control; a hypnotist could usually calm a subject in only seconds. Apparently, Laura had lived through an extremely traumatic fire or had lost a loved one in a blaze. Carol wanted to pursue the matter and learn what was at the root of it, but this wasn't the right time. After taking so long to quiet her patient, she knew the session should be ended quickly.

When Laura was seated in the wing chair again, Carol crouched beside her and instructed her to remember everything that had happened and everything that had been said during the session. Then she led the girl forward through time to the present and brought her out of the trance.

The girl wiped at the moist corner of one eye, shook her head, cleared her throat. She looked at Carol and said, "I guess it didn't work, huh?" She sounded like Jane again; the Laura voice was gone.

But why the hell had her voice changed in the first place? Carol wondered.

"You don't remember what happened?" Carol asked.

"What's to remember? All that talk about a blue kite? I could see what you were trying to do, how you were trying to lull me into a trance, so I guess that's why it didn't work."

"But it *did* work," Carol assured her. "And you should be able to recall all of it."

The girl looked skeptical. "All of what? What happened? What did you find out?"

Carol stared at her. "Laura."

The girl didn't even blink. She merely looked perplexed.

"Your name is Laura."

"Who said?"

"You did."

"Laura? No. I don't think so."

"Laura Havenswood," Carol said.

The girl frowned. "It doesn't ring any bells at all."

Surprised, Carol said, "You told me you live in Shippensburg."

"Where's that?"

"About an hour from here."

"I never heard of it."

"You live on a farm. There are stone gateposts to mark the entrance to your father's property, and there's a long driveway flanked by maple trees. That's what you told me, and I'm sure it'll turn out to be just like you said. It's virtually impossible to answer questions incorrectly or deceptively while you're hypnotized. Besides, you don't have any reason to deceive me. You have nothing to lose and everything to gain if we break through this memory block."

"Maybe I *am* Laura Havenswood," the girl said. "Maybe what I told you in the trance was true. But I can't remember it, and when you tell me who I am, it doesn't mean a thing to me. Boy, I thought if I could just remember my name, then everything would fall into place. But it's still a blank. Laura, Shippensburg, a farm—I can't *connect* with any of it."

Carol was still crouched beside the girl's chair. She rose and flexed her stiff legs. "I've never encountered anything quite like this. And so far as I know, a reaction like yours hasn't ever been reported in any of the psychology journals. Whenever a patient *is* susceptible to hypnosis, and whenever a patient *can* be regressed to a moment of trauma, there's always a profound effect. Yet you weren't touched at all by it. Very odd. If you remembered while you were under hypnosis, you ought to be able to remember now. And just hearing your name ought to open doors for you."

"But it doesn't."

"Strange..."

The girl looked up from the wing chair. "What now?"

Carol thought for a moment, then said, "I suppose we ought to have the authorities check out the Havenswood identity."

She went to her desk, picked up the phone, and called the Harrisburg police.

The police operator referred her to a detective named Lincoln Werth, who was in charge of a number of conventional missing-persons files as well as the Jane Doe case. He listened to Carol's story with interest, promised to check it out right away, and said he would call her back the instant he obtained confirmation of the Havenswood identity.

●II●II●

Four hours later, at 3:55, after Carol's last appointment for the day, as she and the girl were about to leave the office and go home, Lincoln Werth rang back as promised. Carol took the call at her desk, and the girl perched on the edge of the desk, watching, clearly a bit tense.

"Dr. Tracy," Werth said, "I've been back and forth on the phone all afternoon with the police in Shippensburg and with the county sheriff's office up there. I'm afraid I have to report it's all been a wild-goose chase."

"There must be some mistake."

"Nope. We can't find anyone in Shippensburg or the surrounding county with the name Havenswood. There's no telephone listed for anyone of that name, and—"

"Maybe they just don't have a phone."

"Of course, we considered that possibility," Werth

said. "We didn't jump to conclusions, believe me. For instance, when we checked with the power company, we discovered they don't have a customer named Havenswood anywhere in Cumberland County, but that didn't discourage us either. We figured these people we're looking for might be Amish. Lots of Amish in that neck of the woods. If they were Amish, of course, they wouldn't have electricity in their house. So next we went to the property-tax rolls at the county offices up there. What we found was that nobody named Havenswood owns a house, let alone a farm, in that whole area."

"They could be tenants," Carol said.

"Could be. But what I really think they are is non-existent. The girl must've been lying."

"Why would she?"

"I don't know. Maybe the whole amnesia thing is a hoax. Maybe she's just an ordinary runaway."

"No. Definitely not." Carol looked up at Laura— no, her name was still Jane—looked into those clear, bottomless blue eyes. To Werth, she said, "Besides, it just isn't possible to lie that well or that blatantly when you're hypnotized."

Although Jane could hear only half of the conversation, she had begun to perceive that the Havenswood name wasn't going to check out. Her face clouded. She got up and went to the display shelves to study the statuettes of Mickey Mouse.

"There *is* something damned odd about the whole thing," Lincoln Werth said.

"Odd?" Carol asked.

"Well, when I passed along the description of the farm that the girl gave—those stone gateposts, the long driveway with the maples—and when I said it was off Walnut Bottom Road, the Cumberland County sheriff and the various Shippensburg policemen I talked to all recognized the place right off the bat. It actually does exist."

"Well, then—"

"But nobody named Havenswood lives there," Detective Werth said. "The Ohlmeyer family owns that spread. Really well known around those parts. Highly thought of, too. Oren Ohlmeyer, his wife, and their two sons. Never had a daughter, so I'm told. Before Oren owned the farm, it belonged to his daddy, who bought it seventy years ago. One of the sheriff's men went out there and asked the Ohlmeyers if they'd ever heard of a girl named Laura Havenswood or anything even similar to that. They hadn't. Didn't know anyone fitting our Jane Doe's description, either."

"Yet the farm *is* there, just like she told us it was."

"Yeah," Werth said. "Funny, isn't it?"

●‖●‖●

In the Volkswagen, on the way home from the office, as they drove along the sun-splashed autumn streets, the girl said, "Do you think I was faking the trance?"

"Heavens, no! You were *very* deeply under. And I'm quite sure you aren't a good enough actress to fake that business about the fire."

"Fire?"

"I guess you don't remember that, either." Carol told her about Laura's screaming fit, the desperate cries for help. "Your terror was genuine. It came from experience. I'd bet anything on that."

"I don't remember any of it. You mean I really was in a fire once?"

"Could be." Ahead, a traffic light turned red. Carol

stopped the car and looked at Jane. "You don't have any physical scars, so if you were in a fire, you escaped unharmed. Of course, it might be that you *lost* someone in a fire, someone you loved very much, and maybe you weren't actually in a fire yourself. If that's the case, then when you were hypnotized, you might have confused your fear for that person with fear for your own life. Am I making myself clear?"

"I think I get what you mean. So maybe the fire—the *shock* of it—is responsible for my amnesia. And maybe my parents haven't shown up to claim me because... they're dead, burned to death."

Carol took the girl's hand. "Don't worry about it now, honey. I may be all wrong. I probably am. But I think it's a possibility you ought to be prepared for."

The girl bit her lip, nodded. "The idea scares me a little. But I don't exactly feel sad. I mean, I don't remember my folks at all, so losing them would almost be like losing strangers."

Behind them, the driver of a green Datsun blew his horn.

The light had changed. Carol let go of the girl's hand and touched the accelerator. "We'll probe into the fire during tomorrow's session."

"You still think I *am* Laura Havenswood?"

"Well, for the time being, we'll keep calling you Jane. But I don't see why you'd come up with the name Laura if it wasn't yours.".

"The identity didn't check out," the girl reminded her.

Carol shook her head. "That's not exactly true. We haven't proved or disproved the Havenswood identity. All we know for sure is that you never lived in Shippensburg. But you must have been there at least once because the farm exists; you've seen it, if only in passing. Apparently, even under hypnosis, even regressed beyond the onset of your amnesia, your memories are tangled. I don't know how that's possible or why. I've never encountered anything quite like it. But we'll work hard at untangling them for you. The problem might lie in the questions I asked and the way I asked them. We'll just have to wait and see."

They rode in silence for a moment, and then the girl said, "I half hope we don't get things untangled too quickly. Ever since you told me about your cabin in the mountains, I've really been looking forward to going up there."

"Oh, you'll get to go. Don't worry about that. We're leaving on Friday, and even if tomorrow's session goes well, we won't be able to untangle this Laura Havenswood thing *that* fast. I warned you, this could be a slow, complicated, frustrating process. I'm surprised we made any progress at all today, and I'll be twice as surprised if we make even half as much headway tomorrow."

"I guess you'll be stuck with me for a while."

Carol sighed and pretended weariness. "Looks that way. Oh, you're such a terrible, terrible, terrible burden. You're just too much to bear." She took one hand off the steering wheel long enough to clutch her heart in a melodramatic gesture that made Jane giggle. "Too much! Oh, oh!"

"You know what?" the girl asked.

"What?"

"I like you, too."

They looked at each other and grinned.

At the next red light, Jane said, "I've got a feeling about the mountains."

"What's that?"

"I have this strong feeling that it's going to be a lot of fun up there. Really exciting. Something special. A real adventure." Her blue eyes were even brighter than usual.

●II●II●

After dinner, Paul suggested they play Scrabble. He set up the board on the game table in the family room, while Carol explained the rules to Jane, who couldn't remember whether or not she had ever played it before.

After winning the starting lottery, Jane went first with a twenty-two-point word that took advantage of a double-count square and the automatic double score for the first word of the game.

BLADE

"Not a bad start," Paul said. He hoped the girl would win, because she got such a kick out of little things like that. The smallest compliment, the most modest triumph delighted her. But he wasn't going to throw the game just to please her; she would have to earn it, by God. He was incapable of giving the match away to anyone; regardless of the kind of game he was playing, he always put as much effort and commitment into it as he put into his work. He didn't *indulge* in leisure activities; he *attacked* them. To Jane, he said, "I have a hunch you're the kind of kid who says she's never played poker before—and quickly proceeds to win every pot in the game."

"Can you bet on Scrabble?" Jane asked.

"You can, but we won't," Paul said.

"Scared?"

"Terrified. You'd wind up with the house."

"I'd let you stay."

"How decent of you."

"For very low rent."

"Ah, this child truly has a heart of gold!"

While he bantered with Jane, Carol studied her own group of letters. "Hey," she said, "I've got a word that ties right in with Jane's." She added LOOD to the B in BLADE, forming BLOOD.

"Judging from your words," Paul said, "I guess you two intend to play a cutthroat game."

Carol and Jane groaned dutifully at his bad joke and refilled their letter trays from the stock in the lid of the game box.

To Paul's surprise, when he looked at his own seven letters, he saw that he had a word with which to continue the morbid theme that had been established. He added EATH to the D at the end of BLOOD, creating DEATH.

"Weird," Carol said.

"Here's something weirder still," Jane said, taking her second turn by adding OMB to the T in DEATH.

```
B  L  A  D  E
L
O
O
D  E  A  T  H
         O
         M
         B
```

Paul stared at the board. He was suddenly uneasy. What were the odds that the first four words in a game would be so closely related in theme? Ten thousand to one? No. It had to be much higher than that. A hundred thousand to one? A million to one?

Carol looked up from her unusual letters. "You aren't going to *believe* this." She added three letters to the board.

```
              B L A D E
        K I L L
              O
              O
              D E A T H
                  O
                  M
                  B
```

"'Kill'?" Paul said. "Oh, come on. Enough's enough. Take it away and make another word."

"I can't," Carol said. "That's all I have. The rest of my letters are useless."

"But you could have put 'lik' above the 'e' in 'blade,'" Paul said. "You could have spelled 'like' instead of 'kill.'"

"Sure, I could have done that, but I'd have gotten fewer points if I had. You see? There's no square with a double-letter score up there."

As he listened to Carol's explanation, Paul felt strange. Bitterly cold inside. Hollow. As if he were balancing on a tightrope and knew he was going to fall and fall and fall ...

He was gripped by déjà vu, by such a strikingly powerful awareness of having lived through this scene before that, for a moment, his heart seemed to stop beating. Yet nothing like this had ever happened in any other Scrabble game he'd ever played. So why was he so certain he had witnessed this very thing on a previous occasion? Even as he asked himself that question, he realized what the answer was. The seizure of déjà vu wasn't in reference to the words on the Scrabble board; not directly anyway. The thing that was so frighteningly familiar to him was the unusual, soul-shaking *feeling* that the coincidental appearance of those words aroused in him; the iciness that came from within rather than from without; the awful hollowness deep in his guts; the sickening sensation of teetering on a high wire, with only infinite darkness below. He had felt exactly the same way in the attic last week, when the mysterious hammering sound had seemed to issue out of the thin air in front of his face, when each *thunk!* had sounded as if it were coming from a sledge and anvil in another dimension of time and space. That was how he felt now, at the Scrabble board: as if he were confronted with something extraordinary, unnatural, perhaps even supernatural.

To Carol, he said, "Listen, why don't you just take those last three letters off the board, put them back in the box, choose three brand-new letters, and make some other word besides 'kill.'"

He could see that his suggestion startled her.

She said, "Why should I do that?"

Paul frowned. "Blade, blood, death, tomb, kill—what kind of words are they for a nice, friendly, peaceable game of Scrabble?"

She stared at him for a moment, and her piercing eyes made him a bit uncomfortable. "It's only coincidence," she said, clearly puzzled by his tenseness.

"I *know* it's only coincidence," he said, though he didn't know anything of the sort. He was simply un-

able to explain rationally the eerie feeling that the
words on the board were the work of some force far
stronger than mere coincidence, something worse.
"It still gives me the creeps," he said lamely. He
turned to Jane, seeking an ally. "Doesn't it give you
the creeps?"

"Yeah. It does. A little," the girl agreed. "But it's
also kind of fascinating. I wonder how long we can
keep going with words that fit this pattern."

"I wonder, too," Carol said. Playfully, she slapped
Paul's shoulder. "You know what your trouble is,
babe? You don't have any scientific curiosity. Now
come on. It's your turn."

After putting DEATH on the board, he hadn't re-
plenished his supply of letter tiles. He drew four of
the small wooden squares from the lid of the game
box, put them on the rack in front of him.

And froze.

Oh God.

He was on that tightrope again, teetering over a
great abyss.

"Well?" Carol asked.

Coincidence. It *had* to be just coincidence.

"Well?"

He looked up at her.

"What have you got?" she asked.

Numb, he shifted his eyes to the girl.

She was hunched over the table, as eager as Carol
to hear his response, anxious to see if the macabre
pattern would continue.

Paul lowered his eyes to the row of letters on the
wooden rack. The word was still there. Impossible.
But it was there anyway, possible or not.

"Paul?"

He moved so quickly and unexpectedly that Carol and Jane jumped. He scooped up the letters on his rack and nearly flung them back into the lid of the box. He swept the five offensive words off the board before anyone could protest, and he returned those nineteen tiles to the box with all the others.

"Paul, for heaven's sake!"

"We'll start a new game," he said. "Maybe those words didn't bother you, but they bothered me. I'm here to relax. If I want to hear about blood and death and killing, I can switch on the news."

Carol said, "What word did you have?"

"I don't know," he lied. "I didn't work with the letters to see. Come on. Let's start all over."

"You *did* have a word," she said.

"No."

"It looked to me like you did," Jane said.

"Open up," Carol said.

"All right, all right. I had a word. It was obscene. Not something a gentleman like me would use in a refined game of Scrabble, with ladies present."

Jane's eyes sparkled mischievously. "Really? Tell us. Don't be stuffy."

"Stuffy? Have you no manners, young lady?"

"None!"

"Have you no modesty?"

"Nope."

"Are you just a common *broad*?"

"Common," she said, nodding rapidly. "Common to the core. So tell us what word you had."

"Shame, shame, shame," he said. Gradually, he cajoled them into dropping their inquiry. They started a new game. This time all the words were ordinary, and they did not come in any unsettling, related order.

●II●II●

Later, in bed, he made love to Carol. He wasn't particularly horny. He just wanted to be as close to her as he could get.

Afterwards, when the murmured love talk finally faded into a companionable silence, she said, "What *was* your word?"

"Hmmmm?" he said, pretending not to know what she meant.

"Your obscene word in the Scrabble game. Don't try to tell me you've forgotten what it was."

"Nothing important."

She laughed. "After everything we just did in this bed, surely you don't think I need to be sheltered!"

"I didn't have an obscene word." Which was the truth. "I didn't really have any word at all." Which was a lie. "It's just that . . . I thought those first five words on the board were bad for Jane."

"Bad for her?"

"Yes. I mean, you told me it's quite possible she lost one or both of her parents in a fire. She might be on the brink of learning about or remembering a terrible tragedy in her recent past. Tonight she just needed to relax, to laugh a bit. How could the game have been fun for her if the words on the board started to remind her that her parents might be dead?"

Carol turned on her side, raised herself up a bit, leaned over him, her bare breasts grazing his chest, and stared into his eyes. "Is that really the only reason you were so upset?"

"Don't you think I was right? Did I overreact?"

"Maybe you did. Maybe you didn't. It *was* creepy." She kissed his nose. "You know why I love you so much?"

"Because I'm such a great lover?"

"You are, but that's not why I love you."

"Because I have tight buns?"

"Not that."

"Because I keep my fingernails so neat and clean?"

"Not that."

"I give up."

"You're so damned sensitive, so caring about other people. How typical of my Paul to worry about the Scrabble game being fun for Jane. *That's* why I love you."

"I thought it was my hazel eyes."

"Nah."

"My classic profile."

"Are you kidding?"

"Or the way my third toe on my left foot lays half under the second toe."

"Oh, I'd forgotten about that. Hmmmmm. You're right. *That's* why I love you. Not because you're sensitive. It's your *toes* that drive me wild."

Their teasing led to cuddling, and the cuddling led to kissing, and the kissing led to passion again. She reached her peak only a few seconds before he spurted deep within her, and when they finally parted for the night, he felt pleasantly wrung out.

Nevertheless, she was asleep before he was. He stared at the dark ceiling of the dark bedroom and thought about the Scrabble game.

BLADE, BLOOD, DEATH, TOMB, KILL...

He thought about the word he had hidden from Carol and Jane, the word that had compelled him to end the game and start another. After adding EATH to the D in BLOOD, he'd been left with just three letter tiles on his rack: X, U, and C. The X and the

U had played no part in what was to follow. But when he had drawn four new letters, they had gone disconcertingly well with the C. First he'd picked up an A, then an R. And he had known what was going to happen. He hadn't wanted to continue; he'd considered throwing all the tiles back into the box at that moment, for he dreaded seeing the word that he knew the last two letters would spell. But he hadn't ended it there. He had been too curious to stop when he should have stopped. He had drawn a third tile, which had been an O, and then a fourth, L.

C...A...R...O...L...

BLADE, BLOOD, DEATH, TOMB, KILL, CAROL.

Of course, even if he was able to fit it in, he couldn't put CAROL on the board, for it was a proper name, and the rules didn't allow the use of proper names. But that was a moot point. The important thing was that her name had been spelled out so neatly, so boldly on his rack of letters that it was uncanny. He had drawn the letters in their proper order, for God's sake! What were the odds against *that*?

It seemed to be an omen. A warning that something was going to happen to Carol. Just as Grace Mitowski's two nightmares had turned out to be prophetic.

He thought about the other strange events that had transpired recently: the unnaturally violent lightning strikes at Alfred O'Brian's office; the hammering sound that had shaken the house; the intruder on the rear lawn during the thunderstorm. He sensed that all of it was tied together. But for Christ's sake, *how*?

BLADE, BLOOD.
DEATH, TOMB.

KILL, CAROL.

If the series of words on the Scrabble tiles had
constituted a prophetic warning, what was he supposed to do about it? The omen, if it *was* an omen,
was too vague to have any value. There was nothing
specific to guard against. He couldn't protect Carol
until he knew from which direction the danger was
coming. A car wreck? A plane crash. A mugger?
Cancer? It could be anything. He could see nothing
to be gained by telling Carol that her name had turned
up on his rack of Scrabble tiles; there was nothing she
could do, either, nothing except worry about it.

He didn't want to worry her.

Instead, lying in the darkness, feeling icy even
under the covers, he worried *for* her.

●‖●‖●

At two o'clock in the morning, Grace was still reading
in the study. There wasn't any point in going to bed
for at least another hour or two. The events of the last
week had turned her into an insomniac.

The day just past had been relatively uneventful.
Aristophanes was still behaving oddly—hiding from
her, sneaking about, watching her when he thought
she didn't know he was there—but he hadn't torn up
any more pillows or furniture, and he had used his
litter box as he was supposed to do, which were en-
couraging signs. She hadn't received any more telephone calls from the man who had pretended to be
Leonard, and for that she was grateful. Yes, it had
been pretty much an ordinary day.

And yet...

She was still tense and unable to sleep because she

sensed that she was in the eye of the hurricane. She sensed that the peace and quiet in her house were deceptive, that thunder and lightning raged on all sides of her, just beyond the range of her hearing and just out of sight. She expected to be plunged back into the storm at any moment, and that expectation made it impossible for her to relax.

She heard a furtive sound and glanced up from the novel she was reading.

Aristophanes appeared at the open study door, peering in from the hallway. Only his elegant Siamese head was visible as he craned it cautiously around the doorframe.

Their eyes met.

For an instant, Grace felt that she was not looking into the eyes of a dumb animal. They seemed to contain intelligence. Wisdom. Experience. More than mere animal intent and purpose.

Aristophanes hissed.

His eyes were cold. Twin balls of crystal-clear, blue-green ice.

"What do you want, cat?"

He broke the staring contest. He turned away from her with haughty indifference, padded past the doorway, and went softly down the hall, pretending that he hadn't been spying on her, even though they both knew he had been doing exactly that.

Spying? she thought. Am I crazy? Who would a cat be spying for? Catsylvania? Great Kitten? Purrsia?

She could think of other puns, but none of them brought a smile to her lips.

Instead, she sat with the book on her lap, wondering about her sanity.

9

THURSDAY AFTERNOON.

The office drapes were tightly closed as usual. The light from the two floor lamps was golden, diffuse. Mickey Mouse was still smiling broadly in all his many incarnations.

Carol and Jane sat in the wing chairs.

The girl slipped into a trance with only a little assistance from Carol. Most patients were more susceptible to hypnosis the second time than they had been the first, and Jane was no exception.

Again using the imaginary wristwatch, Carol turned the hands of time backwards and regressed Jane into the past. This time the girl didn't need two minutes to get beyond her amnesia. In only twenty or thirty seconds, she reached a point at which memories existed for her.

She twitched and suddenly sat up ramrod-straight in her chair. Her eyes popped open like the eyes on a doll; she was looking *through* Carol. Her face was twisted with terror.

"Laura?" Carol asked.

Both of the girl's hands flew up to her throat. She clutched herself, gasping, gagging, grimacing in pain. She appeared to be reliving the same traumatic experience that had panicked her during yesterday's sessions, but today she did not scream.

"You can't feel the fire," Carol told her. "There is no pain, honey. Relax. Be calm. You can't smell the smoke, either. It doesn't bother you at all. Breathe easily, normally. Be calm and relax."

The girl didn't obey. She quivered and broke out in a sweat. She retched repeatedly, dryly, violently, yet almost silently.

Afraid that she had lost control again, Carol redoubled her efforts to soothe her patient, without success.

Jane began to gesture wildly, her hands cutting and stabbing and tugging and hammering at the air.

Abruptly, Carol realized the girl was trying to talk, but for some reason had lost her voice.

Tears welled up and slid down Jane's face. She was moving her mouth without the slightest result, desperately trying to force out words that refused to come. In addition to the terror in her eyes, there was now frustration.

Carol quickly fetched a notebook and a felt-tipped pen from her desk. She put the notebook on Jane's lap and pressed the pen into her hand.

"Write it for me, honey."

The girl squeezed the pen so hard that her knuckles were white and nearly as sharp as the knuckles on a skeleton's fleshless hand. She looked down at the notebook. She stopped retching, but she continued to quiver.

Carol crouched beside the wing chair, where she could see the notebook. "What is it you want to say?"

Her hand shaking like that of a palsied old woman, Jane hurriedly scrawled two words that were barely legible: *Help me.*

"Why do you need help?"

Again: *Help me.*

"Why can't you speak?"

Head.

"Be more specific."

My head.

"What about your head?"

The girl's hand began to form a letter, then jumped down one line and made another false start, jumped to a third line— as if she couldn't figure out how to express what she wanted to say. At last, in a frenzy, she started slashing at the paper with the felt-tipped pen, making a meaningless crosshatching of black lines.

"Stop it!" Carol said. "You *will* relax, dammit. Be calm."

Jane stopped slashing at the paper. She was silent, staring down at the notebook on her lap.

Carol tore off the smeared page and threw it on the floor. "Okay. Now you're going to answer my questions calmly and as fully as you can. What is your name?"

Millie.

Carol stared at the handwritten name, wondering what had happened to Laura Havenswood. "Millie? Are you sure that's your name?"

Millicent Parker.

"Where is Laura?"

Who's Laura?

Carol stared at the girl's drawn face. The perspiration was beginning to dry on her porcelain-smooth skin. Her blue eyes were blank, unfocused. Her mouth was slack.

Carol abruptly flashed a hand past the girl's face. Jane didn't flinch. She wasn't faking the trance.

"Where do you live, Millicent?"

Harrisburg.

"Right here in town. What's your address?"

Front Street.

"Along the river? Do you know the number?"

The girl wrote it down.

"What's your father's name?"

Randolph Parker.

"What's your mother's name?"

The pen made a meaningless squiggle on the notebook page.

"What's your mother's name?" Carol repeated.

The girl surrendered to a new series of spasmic tremors. She retched soundlessly and put her hands to her throat once more. The felt-tipped pen made a black mark on the underside of her chin.

Apparently, the mere mention of her mother frightened her. That was territory that would have to be explored, though not right now.

Carol talked her down, calmed her, and asked a new question. "How old are you, Millie?"

Tomorrow's my birthday.

"Is it really? How old will you be?"

I won't make it.

"What won't you make?"

Sixteen.

"Are you fifteen now?"

Yes.

"And you think you won't live to be sixteen? Is that it?"

Won't live.

"Why not?"

The sheen of sweat had nearly evaporated from the girl's face, but again perspiration popped out along her hairline.

"Why won't you live to see your birthday?" Carol persisted.

As before, the girl used the felt-tipped pen to slash angrily at the notebook.

"Stop that," Carol said firmly. "Relax and be calm and answer my question." She tore the ruined page out of the book and tossed it aside, then said, "Why won't you live to see your sixteenth birthday, Millie?"

Head.

So we're back to this, Carol thought. She said, "What about your head? What's wrong with it?"

Cut off.

Carol stared at those two words for a moment, then looked up at the girl's face.

Millie-Jane was struggling to remain calm, as Carol had told her she must. But her eyes jiggled nervously, and there was horror in them. Her lips were utterly colorless, tremulous. Beneath the rivulets of sweat that coursed down her forehead, her skin was waxy and mealy white.

She continued to scribble frantically in the notebook, but all she wrote was the same thing over and over again: *Cut off, cut off, cut off, cut off...* She was bearing down on the page with such great pressure that the head of the felt-tipped pen was squashed into shapeless mush.

My God, Carol thought, this is like a live report from the bottom of Hell.

Laura Havenswood. Millicent Parker. One girl screaming in pain as fire consumed her, the other a victim of decapitation. What did either of those girls have to do with Jane Doe? She couldn't be *both* of them. Perhaps she wasn't either of them. Were they people she had known? Or were they only figments of her imagination?

What in Christ's name is happening here? Carol wondered.

She put her own hand over the girl's writing hand and stilled the squeaking pen. Speaking gently, rhythmically, she told Millie-Jane that everything was all right, that she was perfectly safe, and that she must relax.

The girl's eyes stopped jiggling. She sagged back in her chair.

"All right," Carol said. "I think that's enough for today, honey."

Employing the imaginary wristwatch, she brought the girl forward in time.

For a few seconds everything went well, but then, without warning, the girl erupted from her chair, knocking the notebook off her lap and flinging the pen across the room. Her pale face flushed red, and her placid expression gave way to a look of pure rage.

Carol rose from beside the girl's chair and stepped in front of her. "Honey, what's wrong?"

The girl's eyes were wild. She began to shout with such force that she sprayed Carol with spittle. "Shit! The bitch did it! The rotten, goddamn bitch!"

The voice wasn't Jane's.

It wasn't Laura's either.

It was a new voice, a third one, with its own special character, and Carol had a hunch it didn't belong to Millicent Parker, the mute. She suspected that an entirely new identity had surfaced.

The girl stood very stiff and straight, her hands fisted at her sides, staring off into infinity. Her face was distorted by anger. "The stinking bitch did it! She did it to me *again*!"

The girl continued to shout at the top of her voice, and half of the words she blurted out were obscene. Carol tried to soothe her, but this time it wasn't easy. For at least a minute the girl continued to wail and curse. At last, however, at Carol's urging, she got control of herself. She stopped shouting, but there was still anger in her face.

Holding the girl by the shoulders, face to face with her, Carol said, "What's your name?"

"Linda."

"What's your last name?"

"Bektermann."

It was yet another identity, as Carol had thought. She had the girl spell the name.

Then: "Where do you live, Linda?"

"Second Street."

"In Harrisburg?"

"Yes."

Carol asked for the exact address, and the girl responded. It was only a few blocks from the Front Street address that Millicent Parker had provided.

"What's your father's name, Linda?"

"Herbert Bektermann."

"What's your mother's name?"

That question had the same effect on Linda as it had had on Millie. She rapidly became agitated and began to shout again. "The bitch! Oh, God, what she *did* to me. The slimy, rotten bitch! I hate her. I hate her!"

Chilled by the combination of fury and agony in the girl's tortured voice, Carol quickly quieted her.

Then: "How old are you, Linda?"

"Tomorrow's my birthday."

Carol frowned. "Am I talking to Millicent now?"

"Who's Millicent?"

"Is this still Linda I'm talking to?"

"Yes."

"And your birthday is tomorrow?"

"Yes."

"How old will you be?"

"I won't make it."

Carol blinked. "You mean you won't live to see your birthday?"

"That's right."

"Is it your sixteenth birthday?"

"Yes."

"You're fifteen now?"

"Yes."

"Why are you worried about dying?"

"Because I know I will."

"How do you know?"

"Because I already am."

"You're already dying?"

"Dead."

"You're already dead?"

"I will be."

"Please be specific. Are you telling me that you're already dead? Or are you saying that you're merely afraid you're *going* to die sometime soon?"

"Yes."

"Which is it?"

"Both."

Carol felt as if she were in the middle of a tea party at the Mad Hatter's house.

"How do you think you're going to die, Linda?"

"She'll kill me."

"Who?"

"The bitch."

"Your mother?"

The girl doubled over and clutched at her side, as if she had been struck. She screamed, turned, staggered two steps, and fell with a crash. On the floor she still clutched her side, and she kicked her legs, writhed. She was obviously in unendurable pain. It was only imaginary pain, of course, but to the girl it was indistinguishable from the real thing.

Frightened, Carol knelt beside her, held her hand, and urged her to be calm. When the girl eventually relaxed, Carol quickly brought her all the way back to the present and out of the trance.

Jane blinked, stared up at Carol, and put one hand on the floor beside her, as if testing the truth of what her eyes told her. "Wow, what am I doing down here?"

Carol helped her to her feet. "I suppose you don't remember?"

"No. Did I tell you anything more about myself?"

"No. I don't think so. You told me you were a girl named Millicent Parker, and then you told me you were a girl named Linda Bektermann, but obviously you can't be *both* of them *and* Laura, too. So I suspect that you aren't any of them."

"I don't think so, either," Jane said. "Those two new names don't mean anything more to me than Laura Havenswood did. But who *are* those people? Where did I get their names, and why did I tell you I was any of them?"

"I'll be damned if I know," Carol said. "But sooner or later, we'll figure it out. We'll get to the bottom of all this, kiddo. I promise you that."

But what in God's name will we find at the bottom, down there in the dark? Carol wondered. Will it be something we'll wish we'd left buried forever?

●ll●ll●

Thursday afternoon, Grace Mitowski worked in the rose garden behind her house. The day was warm and clear, and she felt the need for some exercise. Besides, in the garden she wouldn't be able to hear the telephone ringing and wouldn't be tempted to answer it. Which was fine, because she wasn't psychologically prepared to answer the phone just yet; she hadn't decided how to deal with the hoaxer the next time he called and pretended that he was her long-dead husband.

Because of last week's torrential rains, the roses were past their prime. The last flowers of the season should have been at the peak of their beauty right now, but many of the big blooms had lost a fifth or even a fourth of their petals under the lashing of the wind-whipped rain. Nevertheless, the garden was still a colorful, cheery sight.

She had let Aristophanes out for some exercise.

She kept an eye on him, intending to call him back the moment he headed off the property. She was determined to keep him away from whoever had poisoned or drugged him. But he didn't seem to be in a rambling mood; he stayed nearby, creeping among the roses, stirring up a moth or two and chasing them with catlike singlemindedness.

Grace was on her hands and knees in front of a row of intermingled yellow and crimson and orange flowers, hand-spading the earth with a trowel, when someone said, "You have a magnificent garden."

Startled, she looked up and saw a thin, jaundice-skinned man in a rumpled blue suit that hadn't been in fashion for many years. His shirt and tie were hopelessly out of style, too. He looked as if he had stepped out of a photograph taken in the 1940s. He had thinning hair the color of summer dust, and his eyes were an unusual shade of soft brown, almost beige. His face was composed entirely of narrow features and sharp angles that gave him a look halfway between that of a hawk and that of a parsimonious moneylender in a Charles Dickens novel. He appeared to be in his early or middle fifties.

Grace glanced at the gate in the white board fence that separated her property from the street. The gate was standing wide open. Evidently, the man had been strolling by, had seen the roses through a gap in the poplar-tree hedge that stood on the outside of the fence, and had decided to come in and have a closer look.

His smile was warm, and there was kindness in his eyes, and he seemed not to be intruding, even though he was. "You must have two dozen varieties of roses here."

"Three dozen," she said.

"Truly magnificent," he said, nodding approval. His voice wasn't thin and sharp like the rest of him. It was deep, mellow, friendly, and would have seemed more fitting if it had issued from a brawny, hearty fellow half again this man's size. "You take care of the entire garden yourself?"

Grace sat back on her heels, still holding the trowel in one gloved hand. "Sure. I enjoy it. And somehow . . . it just wouldn't be *my* garden if I hired someone to help me with it."

"Exactly!" the stranger said. "Yes, I can understand how you feel."

"Are you new in the neighborhood?" Grace asked.

"No, no. Used to live just a block from here, but that was a long, long time ago." He took a deep breath and smiled again. "Ah, the wonderful aroma of roses! Nothing else smells half so pretty. Yes, you've got a superb garden. Really superb."

"Thank you."

He snapped his fingers as a thought occurred to him. "I ought to write something about this. It might make a first-rate human-interest piece. This fantasyland tucked away in an ordinary backyard. Yes, I'm sure it would be just the thing. A nice change of pace for me."

"Are you a writer?"

"Reporter," he said, still taking deep breaths and savoring the aroma of the blooms.

"Are you with a local paper?"

"The *Morning News*. Name's Palmer Wainwright."

"Grace Mitowski."

"I hoped you might recognize my byline," Wainwright said, grinning.

"Sorry. I don't read the *Morning News*. I take the *Patriot-News* from the delivery boy every morning."

"Ah, well," he said, shrugging, "that's a good paper, too. But of course, if you don't read the *Morning News,* you never saw my story about the Bektermann case."

As Grace realized that Wainwright intended to hang around awhile, she got off her haunches, stood up, and flexed her rapidly stiffening legs. "The Bektermann case? That sounds familiar."

"All the papers reported it, of course. But I did a five-part series. Good stuff, even if I do say so myself. I got a Pulitzer nomination for it. Did you know that? An honest-to-God Pulitzer nomination."

"Really? Why, that's something," Grace said, not sure if she should take him seriously but not wanting to offend him. "That is *really* something. Imagine. A Pulitzer nomination."

It seemed to her that the conversation had suddenly taken an odd turn. It wasn't casual any longer. She sensed that Wainwright had come into the yard not to admire her roses and not to have a friendly chat, but to tell her, a complete stranger, about his Pulitzer nomination.

"Didn't win," Wainwright said. "But the way I look at it, a nomination is almost as good as the prize itself. I mean, out of the tens of thousands of newspaper articles that're published in a year, only a handful are up for the prize."

"Refresh my memory, if you will," Grace said. "What was the Bektermann case about?"

He laughed good-naturedly and shook his head. "Wasn't about what I *thought* it was about. That's for damned sure. I wrote it up as a tangled, Freudian puzzle. You know—the iron-willed father, with perhaps an unnatural attraction for his own daughter, the mother with a drinking problem, the poor girl caught in the middle. The victimized young girl subjected to hideous psychological pressures beyond her understanding, beyond her tolerance, until at last she simply—*snapped*. That's how I saw it. That's how I wrote it up. I thought I was a brilliant detective, digging to the deepest roots of the Bektermann tragedy. But all I ever saw was the window-dressing. The real story was far stranger than anything I ever imagined. Hell, it was too strange for any serious reporter to risk handling it. No reputable paper would have printed it as news. If I *had* known the truth, and if I *had* somehow gotten it published, I'd have destroyed my career."

What the devil's going on? Grace wondered. He seems obsessed with telling me about this in detail, *compelled* to tell me, even though he's never even seen me before. Is this life imitating art—Coleridge's poem reset in a rose garden? Am I the partygoer and Wainwright the Ancient Mariner?

As she looked into Wainwright's beige eyes, she suddenly realized how alone she was, even here in the yard. Her property was ringed by trees, sheltered, private.

"Was it a murder case?" she asked.

"Was and is," Wainwright said. "It didn't end with the Bektermanns. It's still going on. This damned, endless pursuit. It's still going on, and it's got to be stopped this time around. That's why I'm here. I've come to tell you that your Carol is in the middle of it. Caught in the middle. You've got to help her. Get her out of the girl's way."

Grace gaped at him, reluctant to believe that she had heard what she knew she had heard.

"There are certain forces, dark and powerful forces," Wainwright said calmly, "that want to see—"

Shrieking angrily, Aristophanes sprang at Wainwright with berserk passion. He landed on the man's chest and scrambled onto his face.

Grace screamed and jumped back in fright.

Wainwright staggered to one side, grabbed the cat with both hands, and tried unsuccessfully to wrench it off his face.

"Ari!" Grace cried. "Stop it!"

Aristophanes had his claws in the man's neck and was biting his cheek.

Wainwright wasn't screaming as he ought to have been. He was eerily silent as he wrestled with the cat, even though the creature seemed determined to tear off his face.

Grace moved toward Wainwright, wanting to help, not knowing what to do.

The cat was squealing. It bit off a gobbet of flesh from Wainwright's cheek.

Oh Jesus, no!

Grace moved in quickly, raising the trowel, but hesitated. She was afraid of hitting the man instead of the cat.

Wainwright suddenly turned away from her and stumbled through the rose bushes, past white and yellow blooms, the cat still clinging to him. He walked into a waist-high hedge, fell through it, onto the lawn on the other side, out of sight.

Grace hurried to the end of the hedgerow, stepped around it, heart hammering, and discovered that

Wainwright had vanished. Only the cat was there, and it bolted past her, sprinted across the garden, up the back porch steps, and into the house through the half-open rear door.

Where was Wainwright? Had he crawled away, dazed, wounded? Had he passed out in some sheltered corner of the garden, bleeding to death?

The yard contained half a dozen shrubs large and dense enough to conceal the body of a man Wainwright's size. She looked around all of them, but she could find no trace of the reporter.

She looked toward the garden gate that led to the street. No. He couldn't have gone that far without drawing her attention.

Frightened, confused, Grace blinked at the sun-dappled garden, trying to understand.

●‖●‖●

The Harrisburg telephone book contained neither a listing for Mr. Randolph Parker nor one for Herbert Bektermann. Carol was perplexed but not surprised.

After she saw her final patient of the day, she and Jane drove to the address on Front Street where Millicent Parker had claimed to live. It was a huge, impressive Victorian mansion, but it hadn't been anyone's home for a long time. The front lawn had been paved over for a parking lot. There was a small, tasteful sign by the entrance drive:

MAUGHAM & CRICHTON, INC.
A MEDICAL CORPORATION

Many years ago, this portion of Front Street had been one of the most elegant neighborhoods in Pennsylvania's capital city. During the past couple of decades, however, many of the riverfront boulevard's grand old houses had been razed to make room for sterile, modern office buildings. A few of the rambling houses had been preserved, at least after a fashion—the exteriors beautifully restored, the interiors gutted and converted to various commercial uses. Farther north, there was still a section of Front Street that was a desirable residential area, but not here, not where Millicent Parker had sent them.

Maugham & Crichton was a group medical practice that included seven physicians: two general internists and five specialists. Carol had a chat with the receptionist, a henna-haired woman named Polly, who told her that none of the doctors was named Parker. Likewise, no one of that name was employed as a nurse or as a member of the clerical staff. Furthermore, Maugham & Crichton had been at their current address for nearly seventeen years.

It had occurred to Carol that Jane might once have been a patient of one of Maugham & Crichton's physicians, and that her subconscious mind had made use of the firm's address to flesh out the Millicent Parker identity. But Polly, who had worked for Maugham & Crichton ever since they'd opened their doors, was sure she had never seen the girl. However, intrigued by Jane's amnesia and sympathetic by nature, Polly agreed to check the files to see if Maugham & Crichton had ever treated anyone named Laura Havenswood, Millicent Parker, or Linda Bektermann. It was a fruitless search; none of those names appeared in the patient records.

●Ⅱ●Ⅱ●

Grace stepped through the gate, into the street, and looked both ways. There was no sign of Palmer Wainwright.

She returned to her own backyard, closed and latched the gate, and walked toward the house.

Wainwright was sitting on the porch steps, waiting for her.

She stopped fifteen feet from him, amazed, confused.

He got up from the steps.

"Your face," she said numbly.

His face was unscarred.

He smiled as if nothing had happened and took two steps toward her. "Grace——"

"The cat," she said. "I saw your cheek . . . your neck . . . it's claws tore out . . ."

"Listen," he said, taking another step toward her, "there are certain forces, dark and powerful forces, that want to see this played out the wrong way. Dark forces that thrive on tragedy. They want to see it end in senseless violence and blood. That mustn't be allowed to happen, Grace. Not again. You've got to keep Carol out of the girl's way, for her sake and for the sake of the girl, too."

Grace gaped at him. "Who the hell are you?"

"Who are *you?*" Wainwright asked, raising one eyebrow quizzically. "*That* is the important question right now. You aren't only who you think you are. You aren't only Grace Mitowski."

He's mad, she thought. Or I'm mad. Or we both are. Stark, raving mad.

She said, "You're the one on the phone. You're the creep who imitates Leonard's voice."

"No," he said. "I am——"

"No wonder Ari attacked you. You're the one who's been giving him drugs or poison or something like that. You're the one, and he *knew*."

But what about the facial wounds, the gouged neck? she asked herself. How in the name of God did those injuries heal so quickly?

How?

She pushed those thoughts out of her mind, refused to think about such things. She must have been mistaken. She must have imagined that Ari had actually hurt the man.

"Yeah," she said, "you're the one who's behind all of these weird things that've been happening. Get off my property, you son of a bitch."

"Grace, there are forces aligned..." He looked no different now from the way he had looked when he'd first spoken to her, several minutes ago. He hadn't looked crazed then; he didn't look crazed now. He didn't look dangerous, and yet he continued to babble about dark forces. "...good and evil, right and wrong. You're on the right side, Grace. But the cat— ah, the cat's a different story. At all times, you must be wary of the cat."

"Get out of my way," she said.

He took a step toward her.

She slashed at him with the gardening trowel, missing his face by just an inch or two. She slashed again and again and again, cutting only empty air, not really wanting to cut anything else unless she had no choice, just hoping to keep him at bay until she could slip around him, for he was between her and the house. And then she *was* around him; she turned and ran for the kitchen door, painfully aware that her legs were old and arthritic. She went only a few steps before she realized she shouldn't have turned her back on the lunatic, and she wheeled to confront him, gasping, certain that he was leaping toward her, perhaps with a knife in his hand—

But he was gone.

Vanished. Again.

He hadn't had time to reach any of the shrubs that were large enough to conceal a man, not during the split second her back had been turned. Even if he had been a much younger man than he was, in the very best condition, a trained runner—even then he couldn't have gone more than halfway to the gate in such a short time.

So where was he?

Where was he?

●‖●‖●

From the offices of Maugham & Crichton on Front Street, Carol and Jane drove a few blocks to the Second Street address that was supposed to be the home of Linda Bektermann. It was in a good neighborhood; a lovely French country house, at least fifty years old, in fine condition. No one was at home, but the name on the mailbox was Nicholson, not Bektermann.

They rang the bell at the house next door and talked to a neighbor, Jean Gunther, who confirmed that the French country place was owned and occupied by the Nicholson family.

"My husband and I have lived here for six years," Mrs. Gunther said, "and the Nicholsons were next door when we moved in. I think I once heard them say they'd lived in that house since 1965."

The name Bektermann meant nothing to Jean Gunther.

In the car again, on the way home, Jane said, "I'm really a lot of trouble for you."

"Nonsense," Carol said. "I kind of enjoy playing detective. Besides, if I can help you break through your memory block, if I can uncover the truth behind all the sleight-of-hand tricks that your subconscious is playing, then I'll be able to write about this case for any psychology journal I choose. It'll definitely make my name in the profession. I might even wind up with a book out of it. So you see, because of you, kiddo, I could become rich and famous some day."

"When you're rich and famous, will you still talk to me?" the girl teased.

"Certainly. Of course, you'll have to make an appointment a week in advance."

They grinned at each other.

●II●II●

Using the kitchen phone, Grace called the offices of the *Morning News*.

The switchboard operator at the newspaper didn't have an extension number listed for Palmer Wainwright. She said, "So far as I know, he don't even work here. And I'm sure he's no reporter. Maybe one of the new copy editors or somebody like that."

"Could you connect me with the managing editor's office?" Grace asked.

"That would be Mr. Quincy," the operator said. She buzzed the proper extension.

Quincy wasn't in his office, and his secretary didn't

know whether or not the paper employed a man named Palmer Wainwright. "I'm new here," she said apologetically. "I've only been Mr. Quincy's secretary since Monday, so I don't know everybody yet. If you'll leave your name and number, I'll have Mr. Quincy return your call."

Grace gave her the number and said, "Tell him Dr. Grace Mitowski wishes to speak with him and that I'll only need a few minutes of his time." She seldom used the honorific in front of her name, but it came in handy in cases like this, for a doctor's phone calls were *always* returned.

"Is this an emergency, Dr. Mitowski? I don't think that Mr. Quincy's going to be back until tomorrow morning."

"That'll be good enough," she said. "Have him call me first thing, no matter how early he gets in."

After she hung up, she went to the kitchen and stared out at the rose garden.

How could Wainwright vanish like that?

●‖●‖●

For the third evening in a row, Paul and Carol and Jane prepared dinner together. The girl was fitting in better day by day.

If she stays with us just another week, Paul thought, it'll seem like she's *always* been here.

The salad consisted of hearts of palm and iceberg lettuce. That was followed by eggplant Parmigiana with spaghetti on the side.

As they were starting dessert—small dishes of richly flavored spumoni—Paul said, "Any chance we could postpone the trip to the mountains for two days?"

"Why?" Carol asked

"I'm a bit behind in my writing schedule, and I'm at a very critical point in the book," he said. "I've written two-thirds of the toughest scene in the story, and I hate to leave it unfinished just to go on vacation. I won't enjoy myself. If we left Sunday instead of tomorrow, that would give me time to polish off the end of the chapter. And we'd still have eight days at the cabin."

"Don't look at me," Jane said. "I'm just excess baggage. I'll go wherever you take me, whenever you take me."

Carol shook her head. "Just last week, when Mr. O'Brian said we were compulsive overachievers, we made up our minds to change our ways, didn't we? We've *got* to learn to make time for leisure and not let our work encroach on that."

"You're right," Paul said. "But just this once—" He broke off in midsentence because he saw that Carol was determined. She was rarely intractable, but when she *did* decide not to compromise on an issue, she was about as movable as Gibraltar. He sighed. "Okay. You win. We'll leave tomorrow morning. I'll just bring along the typewriter and the manuscript. I can finish the scene up at the cabin and—"

"Nothing doing," Carol said, emphasizing each word by tapping her spoon against her ice cream dish. "If you bring it along, you won't stop when you've reached the end of the scene you're working on. You'll keep going. You *know* you will. Having the typewriter within easy reach will just be too much of a temptation. You won't be able to resist it. The whole vacation will go down the drain."

"But I just *can't* put that scene on hold for ten days," he said pleadingly. "By the time I get back to it, the tone and the spontanaeity will be lost."

Carol ate a spoonful of spumoni and said, "All right. Here's what we'll do. Jane and I will leave for the mountains first thing in the morning, just as we planned. You stay here, finish your scene, and then drive up to join us whenever you're ready."

He frowned. "I'm not sure that's a good idea."

"Why not?"

"Well, is it really wise for the two of you to go up there alone? I mean, the summer season is over. There aren't going to be many campers in the woods now, and most of the other cabins will be deserted."

"For heaven's sake," Carol said, "there's no Abominable Snowman lurking around in *those* mountains, Paul. We're in Pennsylvania, not Tibet." She smiled. "It's nice to know you're so concerned about us, darling. But we'll be perfectly safe."

●‖●‖●

Later, after Jane had gone to bed, Paul made one last attempt to change Carol's mind, although he knew the effort would be wasted.

He leaned against the frame of the closet door and watched as Carol selected clothes for the suitcases. "Listen, be straight with me, okay?"

"Aren't I always? Straight about what?"

"The girl. Is there any chance she's dangerous?"

Carol turned from the clothes rack and stared at him, obviously surprised by his question. "Jane? Dangerous? Well, a girl as pretty as she is will probably break a lot of hearts over the years. And if cuteness could kill, she'd leave the streets littered with bodies behind her."

He refused to be amused. "I don't want you to be flippant about this. I think it's important. I want you to give it careful thought."

"I don't *need* to give it a lot of thought, Paul. She's lost her memory, sure. But she's a stable, mentally healthy kid. In fact, it takes an *amazingly* stable personality to handle amnesia the way she's handled it. I don't know that I'd do half as well if I were in her shoes right now. I'd either be a nervous wreck or sunk neck-deep in depression. She's resilient, flexible. Resilient and flexible people aren't dangerous."

"Never?"

"Hardly ever. It's the rigid ones who crack."

"But after what's happened in your therapy sessions with her, isn't it reasonable to wonder about what she might be capable of doing?" he asked.

"She's a tortured girl. I believe she's been through a truly terrifying experience, something so awful that she refuses to relive it, even under hypnosis. She obfuscates, misdirects, and holds back vital information, but that doesn't mean she's the least bit dangerous. Just scared. It seems evident to me that she was the victim of either physical or psychological violence at some time in her life. The *victim*, Paul, not the perpetrator."

She carried a few pairs of jeans to the suitcases that were open on the bed.

Paul followed her. "Are you going to continue her therapy while you're at the cabin?"

"Yes. I think it's best to keep chipping away at the wall of confusion she's thrown up."

"No fair."

"Huh?"

"That's work," he said. "I'm not allowed to take *my* work up to the cabin, but *you're* going to work. That's a double standard, Dr. Tracy."

"Double standard, my ass, Dr. Tracy. I'll need only half an hour a day for Jane's therapy. That's a lot different than lugging an IBM Selectric into the piny woods and pounding on the keys ten hours a day. Don't you realize that all the squirrels and deer and bunny rabbits would complain about the noise?"

●II●II●

Later still, when they were in bed and the lights were out, he said, "Hell, I'm letting this book take possession of me. Why *can't* I let the scene lie unfinished for ten days? I might even do a better job with it if I take the time to think about it. I'll come along with you and Jane tomorrow, and I won't bring the typewriter. Okay? I won't even bring a pencil."

"No," Carol said.

"No?"

"When you *do* get to the mountains, I want you to be able to put the book completely out of your mind. I want us to take long walks in the forest. I want us to go boating on the lake and do some fishing and read a couple of books and act like bums who never even heard the word 'work.' If you don't finish that scene before you go, you'll just brood about it during the entire vacation. You won't have a moment's real peace, which means *I* won't have a moment's peace, either. And don't tell me I'm wrong. I know you better than I know myself, buster. You stay here, write the end of that scene, and then join us on Sunday."

She kissed him goodnight, fluffed her pillows, and settled down to sleep.

He lay in the dark, thinking about the words in yesterday's Scrabble game.

```
            B L A D E
      K I L L
            O
            O
      D E A T H
            O
            M
            B
```

And the one word he had refused to reveal: CAROL...

He still didn't think anything would be gained by telling her what the last of those six words had been. What could she do about it other than worry? Nothing. She could do nothing, and he could do nothing. Except wait and see. A threat—if one actually arose—could come from any of ten thousand or a hundred thousand sources. It could come anytime, anywhere. At home or in the mountains. One place was as safe—or as dangerous—as the other.

Anyway, maybe the appearance of those six words *had* been merely coincidence. An incredible but meaningless coincidence.

He stared into the darkness, trying hard to convince himself that there were no such things as spirit messages, omens, and clairvoyant prophecies. Only a week ago, he wouldn't have *needed* convincing.

●||●||●

Blood.

Get it off, scrub it off, every sticky drop of it, wash it off, quickly, quickly, down the drain, every incriminating drop of it, off, before someone finds out, before someone sees and knows what's been done, wash it off, off. . . .

The girl woke in the bathroom, in a fluorescent glare. She had been sleepwalking again.

She was surprised to find that she was nude. Her knee socks, panties, and T-shirt were scattered on the floor around her.

She was standing in front of the sink, scrubbing herself with a wet washcloth. When she looked at her reflection in the mirror, she was briefly paralyzed by what she saw.

Her face was smeared with blood.

Her arms were spattered with blood.

Her sweetly uptilted, bare breasts glistened with blood.

And she knew instantly that it wasn't her own. She had not been slashed or stabbed. *She* was the one who had done the slashing, the stabbing.

Oh God.

She stared at her gruesome reflection, morbidly fascinated by the sight of her blood-moistened lips.

What have I done?

She slowly lowered her gaze along her crimsoned neck, looked down at the reflection of her right nipple, on which hung a very fat, carmine droplet of gore. The gleaming pearl of blood quivered for an instant on the tip of her erect nipple; then it succumbed to gravity and fell away from her.

She pulled her gaze from the mirror, lowered her head to see where the droplet had struck the floor.

There was no blood.

When she looked directly at herself, rather than at her reflection, she discovered that her body was not covered with blood after all. She touched her bare breasts. They were damp because she had been scrubbing them with the washcloth, but the dampness was nothing more than water. Her arms weren't spattered with blood, either.

She squeezed the washcloth. Clear water dripped from it; the cloth bore no grisly stains.

Confused, she raised her eyes to the mirror once more and saw the blood, as before.

She held out her hand. In reality it was not bloody, but in the mirror it was sheathed in a glove of gore.

A vision, she thought. A weird illusion. That's all. I didn't hurt anyone. I didn't spill anyone's blood.

As she struggled to understand what was happening, her mirror image faded, and the glass in front of her turned black. It seemed to have been transformed into a window that looked out onto another dimension, for it reflected nothing that was in the bathroom.

This is a dream, she thought. I'm really snug in bed, where I belong. I'm only dreaming that I'm in the bathroom. I can put a stop to this just by waking up.

On the other hand, if it was a dream, would she be able to feel the cold ceramic floor beneath her bare feet as vividly as she could feel it now? If it was really only a dream, would she be aware of the cold water on her bare breasts?

She shivered.

In the lightless void on the other side of the mirror, something flickered far off in the darkness.

Wake up!

Something silvery. It flashed again and again, back and forth, the image growing steadily larger.

For God's sake, wake up!

She wanted to run. Couldn't.

She wanted to scream. Didn't.

In seconds the flickering object filled the mirror, pushing back the darkness out of which it had come, and then somehow it burst out of the mirror without shattering the glass, exploded out of the void and into the bathroom with one final, murderous swing, and she saw that it was an ax, bearing down on her face, the steel blade gleaming like the finest silver under the fluorescent lights. As the wickedly sharp edge of the ax swept inexorably toward her head, her knees buckled, and she fainted.

●‖●‖●

Near dawn, Jane woke again.

She was in bed. She was nude.

She threw the covers back, sat up, and saw her T-shirt, panties, and knee socks on the floor beside the bed. She dressed quickly.

The house was silent. The Tracys weren't up yet.

Jane hurried quietly down the hallway to the guest bathroom, hesitated on the threshold, then stepped inside and snapped on the lights.

There was no blood, and the mirror above the sink was only an ordinary mirror, reflecting her worried face but contributing no bizarre images of its own.

Okay, she thought, maybe I *was* sleepwalking. And maybe I *was* actually here without any clothes on, trying to scrub nonexistent blood off my body. But the rest of it was just part of the nightmare. It didn't happen. It couldn't. Impossible. The mirror couldn't really *change* like that.

She stared into her own blue eyes. She wasn't sure what she saw in them.

"Who *am* I?" she asked softly.

●II●II●

All week, Grace's sleep—what little she had managed to get between bouts of insomnia—had been dreamless. But tonight she thrashed for hours in the sheets, trying to fight her way out of a nightmare that seemed to last an eternity.

In the dream, a house was on fire. A big, beautifully ornamented Victorian house. She was standing outside the blazing structure, pounding on a pair of slant-set cellar doors and calling a name over and over again. "Laura! Laura!" She knew that Laura was trapped in the cellar of the burning house and that these doors were the only way out, but the doors were latched on the inside. She hammered on the wood with her bare hands until each blow sent a cruel bolt of pain the length of her arms, through her shoulders, and up the back of her neck. She wished desperately that she had an ax or a pry-bar or some other tool with

which she could smash through the cellar doors, but
she had nothing other than her fists, so she pounded
and pounded until her flesh bruised and split and bled,
and she kept on pounding even then, all the while
screaming for Laura. Windows exploded on the second floor, showering glass down over her, but she
didn't turn away from the slant-set cellar doors; she
didn't run. She continued to slam her bloodied fists
into the wood, praying that the girl would answer at
any moment. She ignored the sparks that showered
down on her and threatened to set her gingham dress
afire. She wept, and she coughed when the wind blew
the acrid smoke in her direction, and she cursed the
wood that so easily resisted her fierce but ineffectual
attack.

The nightmare had no climax, no peak of terror.
It simply went on all night long at a continuously
breathless pace until, a few minutes after dawn, Grace
finally wrenched herself out of the hot, clutching arms
of sleep and woke with a wordless cry, flailing at the
mattress.

She sat up on the edge of the bed and held her
throbbing head in her hands.

Her mouth was filled with the taste of ashes and
bile.

The dream had been so vivid that she had even felt
the high-necked, long-sleeved, blue and white gingham
dress binding at her shoulders and across her bust as
she had hammered on the cellar doors. Now, wide
awake, she could *still* feel the dress binding her, even
though she was wearing a loose nightgown, and even
though she had never worn such a dress in her entire
life.

Worse, she could smell the house burning.

The smoke odor lingered so long after she had awakened that she became convinced that her own house was ablaze. Quickly, she pulled on a robe, stepped into her slippers, and went from one room to another, searching for the fire.

There was no fire.

Yet for almost an hour, the stench of burning wood and tar stayed with her.

10

FRIDAY morning at nine o'clock, Paul sat down at his writing desk, picked up the phone, and called Lincoln Werth, the police detective in charge of the Jane Doe case. He told Werth that Carol was taking the girl out of town for a few days of rest and recreation.

"Might as well," Werth said. "We don't have any leads, and I sure don't think this is going to break wide open anytime soon. We keep expanding the search area, of course. At first we just put the kid's photo and description out to authorities in the surrounding counties. When that didn't do us any good, we put it on the wire to police agencies all over the state. Yesterday morning we took another step and wired the same data to seven neighboring states. But I'll tell you something, just between you and me. Even if we expand the search area all the way to Hong

243

Kong, I got a feeling we ain't never going to find anyone who knows the kid. I just have a hunch. We're going to keep coming up empty-handed."

After talking to Werth, Paul went down to the garage, where Carol and Jane were putting their gear in the trunk of the Volkswagen. To spare the girl grief, Paul didn't pass along Werth's pessimistic assessment of the situation. "He said it's all right to leave town for a few days. The court didn't restrict you to Harrisburg. I told him where the cabin is, so if anyone turns up to claim our girl here, the Harrisburg police will contact the county sheriff out that way, and he or one of his deputies will drop by the cabin and let you know you've got to come back."

Carol kissed him goodbye. Jane kissed him, too; hers was a shy, chaste kiss, lightly planted on his cheek, and when she got into the car, she was blushing brightly.

He stood in front of the house and watched them drive away until the red Volkswagen Rabbit was out of sight.

After almost a week of blue skies, clouds had drifted in again. They were flat, slate gray. They matched Paul's mood.

●ıı●ıı●

When the kitchen phone rang, Grace steeled herself for the sound of Leonard's voice. She sat down in the chair at the small built-in desk, reached up, put her hand on the receiver that hung on the wall, let it ring once more, then picked it up. To her relief, it was Ross Quincy, the managing editor of the *Morning*

News, returning the call she'd made late yesterday afternoon.

"You were inquiring about one of our reporters, Dr. Mitowski?"

"Yes. Palmer Wainwright."

Quincy was silent.

"He does work for you, doesn't he?" Grace asked.

"Uh...Palmer Wainwright has been an employee of the *Morning News*, yes."

"I believe he nearly won a Pulitzer Prize."

"Yes. But of course...that was quite a while back."

"Oh?"

"Well, if you know about the Pulitzer nomination, you must know it was for the series he did on the Bektermann murders."

"Yes."

"Which was back in 1943."

"That long ago?"

"Uh...Dr. Mitowski, exactly what is it you wanted to know about Palmer Wainwright?"

"I'd like to talk with him," she said. "We've met, and we have some unfinished business that I'm rather anxious to take care of. It's a...personal matter."

Quincy hesitated. Then: "Are you a long-lost relative?"

"Of Mr. Wainwright's? Oh, no."

"A long-lost friend?"

"No. Not that either."

"Well, then, I guess I don't have to be delicate about this. Dr. Mitowski, I'm afraid that Palmer Wainwright is dead."

"Dead!" she said, astounded.

"Well, surely you realized there was that possibility. He was never a well man, downright sickly. And you've obviously been out of touch with him for a long time."

"Not all that long," she said.

"Must be at least thirty-five years," Quincy said. "He died back in 1946."

The air at Grace's back seemed suddenly colder than it had been an instant ago, as if a dead man had expelled his icy breath against the nape of her neck.

"Thirty-one years," she said numbly. "You must be wrong."

"Not a chance. I was just a green kid back then, a copyboy. Palmer Wainwright was one of my heroes. I took it pretty hard when he went."

"Are we talking about the same man?" Grace asked. "He was quite thin, with sharp features, pale brown eyes, and a rather sallow complexion. His voice was several notes deeper than you'd expect from just looking at him."

"That was Palmer, all right."

"About fifty-five?"

"He was thirty-six when he died, but he did *look* twenty years older," Quincy said. "It was that string of illnesses, one thing right after another, with cancer at the end. It just wore him down, aged him fast. He was a fighter, but he just couldn't hold on any longer."

Thirty-one years in the grave? she thought. But I saw him yesterday. We had a strange conversation in the rose garden. What do you say to that, Mr. Quincy?

"Dr. Mitowski? Are you still there?"

"Yes. Sorry. Listen, Mr. Quincy, I hate to take your valuable time, but this is really important. I believe the Bektermann case had a lot to do with the personal business I wanted to discuss with Mr. Wainwright. But I don't really know anything about those murders. Would you mind telling me what it was all about?"

"Family tragedy," Quincy said. "The Bektermanns' daughter went berserk the day before her sixteenth birthday. Her mind just snapped. Apparently, she got it in her head that her mother intended to kill her before she turned sixteen, which was not true, of course. But she *thought* it was true, and she went after her mother with an ax. Her father and a visiting cousin got in the way, and she killed them. Her mother actually managed to wrench the ax out of the girl's hands. But that didn't stop the kid. She just picked up a fireplace poker and kept coming. When the mother, Mrs. Bektermann, was backed into a corner and was about to have her skull cracked open with the poker, she didn't have any choice but to swing the ax at her daughter. She hit the girl once, in the side. A pretty deep cut. The kid died in the hospital the next day. Mrs. Bektermann only killed in self-defense, and no charges were brought against her, but she felt so guilty about killing her own child that she had a complete breakdown and eventually wound up in an institution."

"And that's the story that won Mr. Wainwright his Pulitzer nomination?"

"Yeah. In the hands of a lot of reporters, the piece would have been nothing but sensationalistic garbage. But Palmer was good. He wrote a sensitive, well-researched study of a family with serious emotional, interpersonal problems. The father was a domineering man who set extremely high standards for his daughter and very likely had an unnatural attraction to her. The mother was always competing with the father for the girl's heart, mind, and loyalty, and when she saw she was losing that battle, she turned to drink. There were extraordinary psychological pressures brought to bear on the daughter, and Palmer made the reader feel and understand those pressures."

She thanked Ross Quincy for his time and consideration. She hung up the phone.

For a while she just sat there, staring at the softly humming refrigerator, trying to make sense of what she had been told. If Wainwright had died in 1946, whom had she talked to in the garden yesterday?

And what did the Bektermann murders have to do with her? With Carol?

She thought of what Wainwright had told her: *This damned, endless pursuit. It's still going on, and it's got to be stopped this time around.... I've come to tell you that your Carol is in the middle of it.... You've got to help her. Get her out of the girl's way.*

She felt she was on the verge of understanding what he had meant. And she was scared.

Even though a number of impossible things had transpired within the past twenty-four hours, she no longer questioned either her sanity or her perceptions. She was sane, perfectly sane, and in command of all her faculties. Senility was not even a remote possibility any longer. She sensed that the explanation for these events was far more frightening, more soul-shattering even than the prospect of senility, which had once terrified her.

She recalled something else that Palmer Wainwright had said yesterday in the garden: *You aren't only who you think you are. You aren't only Grace Mitowski.*

She knew the solution to the puzzle was within her grasp. She sensed a dark knowledge within her, long-forgotten memories waiting to be tapped. She was afraid to tap them, but she knew she must do precisely that, for Carol's sake, and perhaps for her own sake as well.

Suddenly, the air in the kitchen, though still quite clear, reeked of wood and tar smoke. Grace could hear the crackle of fire, although there were no flames here, now, in this place and time.

Her heart pounded frantically, and her mouth turned dry and sour.

She closed her eyes and could see the burning house as vividly as she had seen it in the dream. She could see the cellar doors, and she could hear herself screaming, calling Laura.

She knew it hadn't been only a dream. It had been a memory, lost for ages, surfacing now, reminding her that, indeed, she was not only Grace Mitowski.

She opened her eyes.

The kitchen was hot, stifling.

She felt herself being pulled along by forces she could not comprehend, and she thought: Is this what I want? Do I really want to flow with this and discover the truth and turn my little world upside down? Can I handle it?

The stench of nonexistent smoke grew stronger.

The roar of nonexistent flames grew louder.

I guess there's no turning back now, she thought.

She held her hands up in front of her face and stared at them, amazed. Her flesh had been miraculously disfigured by stigmata. Her hands were bruised, abraded, bloody. There were splinters of wood embedded in her palms, splinters from the cellar doors

on which she had pounded such a long, long time
ago.

● H ● ‖ ●

At ten o'clock, when the phone rang, Paul had been
at his desk, writing, for almost an hour. The work
had just begun to flow smoothly. He snatched up the
receiver and said, a bit impatiently, "Yes?"

An unfamiliar female voice said, "Could I speak
to Dr. Tracy, please?"

"Speaking."

"Oh. Uh . . . no . . . the Dr. Tracy I'm looking for
is a woman."

"It's my wife you want," he said. "She's out of
town for a few days. Can I take a message?"

"Yes, please. Would you tell her that Polly called
from Maugham & Crichton?"

He jotted the name down on a note pad. "And
what's this in reference to?"

"Dr. Tracy was here yesterday afternoon with a
young girl who's suffering from amnesia. . . ."

"Yes," Paul said, suddenly more interested than
he had been. "I know the case."

"Dr. Tracy was asking if we'd ever heard of anyone
named Millicent Parker."

"That's right. She told me about it last evening.
It was another dead end, I gather."

"It seemed to be a dead end yesterday," Polly said,
"but now it turns out that one of our doctors is familiar
with the name. Dr. Maugham himself, in fact."

"Listen, rather than waiting for my wife to call you
back, why don't you just tell *me* what you've come
up with, and I can pass the information along to her."

"Well, sure, why not? See, Dr. Maugham is the senior partner in the practice. He bought this property eighteen years ago and personally oversaw the restoration of the outside and the renovation of the interior. He's a history bug, so it was natural for him to want to know the history of the building he purchased. He says this place was built in 1902 by a man named Randolph Parker. Parker had a daughter named Millicent."

"1902?"

"That's right."

"Interesting."

"You haven't heard the best part," Polly said, the eagerness of a gossip-monger in her voice. "Seems that back in 1905, the night before Millie's sixteenth birthday party, Mrs. Parker was in the kitchen, decorating a big cake for the girl. Millie snuck in behind her and stabbed her in the back four times."

Unthinking, Paul snapped the pencil he'd been holding ever since he'd written Polly's name on the note pad. One broken piece popped out of his hand, spun across the top of the desk, and fell to the floor.

"She stabbed her own mother?" he asked, hoping that he had not heard correctly.

"Isn't that something?"

"Kill her?" he asked numbly.

"No. Dr. Maugham says that according to the newspaper accounts at that time, the girl used a short-bladed knife. It didn't sink in far enough to do really major damage. No vital organs or blood vessels were affected. Louise Parker—that was the mother's name—managed to grab a meat cleaver from a kitchen rack. She tried to hold the girl off with that. But I guess Millie must have been completely off her rocker, 'cause she charged straight at Mrs. Parker again, and Mrs. Parker had to use that cleaver."

"Jesus."

"Yeah," Polly said, obviously enjoying his shocked reaction. "Dr. Maugham says she put that cleaver right into her daughter's throat. Pretty much cut the girl's head clear off. Isn't that a terrible thing? But what else could she do? Just let the kid go on jabbing that knife into her?"

Stunned, Paul thought about yesterday's hypnotic regression therapy session, which Carol had recounted for him in some detail. He remembered the part about how Jane had claimed to be Millicent Parker and had insisted on writing out her answers to questions and had written that she was unable to talk because her head had been cut off.

"Are you still there?" Polly asked.

"Oh. Uh . . . sorry. Is there more to the story?"

"More?" Polly asked. "Wasn't that *enough*?"

"Yes," he said. "You're absolutely right. That was enough. More than enough."

"I don't know if this information is of any help to Dr. Tracy."

"I'm sure it will be."

"I don't see how it could have anything to do with the girl she brought in here with her yesterday."

"Neither do I," Paul said.

"I mean, that girl can't be Millicent Parker. Millicent Parker has been dead for seventy-six years."

●‖●‖●

In the study, Grace stood at her desk, looking down at the open dictionary.

REINCARNATION (rē´-in-kär-nā´-shen), *n*. 1. the doctrine that the soul, upon death of the body, comes back to earth in another body or form. 2. rebirth of the soul in a new body. 3. a new incarnation or embodiment, as of a person.

Bunk? Nonsense? Superstition? Bullshit?

At one time, not long ago, those were all the words she would have used to write her own irreverent definition of reincarnation. But not now. Not any longer.

She closed her eyes, and with only the slightest effort, she was able to bring back the image of the burning house. She wasn't just envisioning it; she was *there*, hammering with her fists on the cellar door. She was not Grace Mitowski now; she was Rachael Adams, Laura's aunt.

The fire scene was not the only part of Rachael's life that she could recall with perfect clarity. She knew the woman's most intimate thoughts, her hopes and dreams and hates and fears, shared her most closely held secrets, for those thoughts and hopes and dreams and fears and secrets had been her own.

She opened her eyes and needed a moment to refocus them on the present-day world.

REINCARNATION

She closed the dictionary.

God help me, she thought, do I really believe it? Can it be true that I've lived before? And that Carol's lived before? And the girl they're calling Jane Doe?

If it *was* true—if she had been permitted to recall

her previous existence as Rachael Adams in order to
save Carol's life in this incarnation—then she was
wasting valuable time.

She picked up the phone to call the Tracys, wondering how in God's name she was going to make
them believe her.

There was no dial tone.

She jiggled the receiver-cradle buttons.

Nothing.

She put the receiver down and followed the cord
around the side of the desk to the wall, to see if it had
come unplugged. It wasn't unplugged; it was *chewed*.
Bitten in two.

Aristophanes.

She remembered other things that Palmer Wainwright had said in the garden: *There are certain
forces, dark and powerful forces, that want to see this
played out the wrong way. Dark forces that thrive on
tragedy. They want to see it end in senseless violence
and blood . . . There are forces aligned . . . good and
evil, right and wrong. You're on the right side, Grace.
But the cat—ah, the cat's a different story. At all
times, you must be wary of the cat.*

She also remembered when the series of paranor-
mal events had begun, and she realized that the cat
had been an integral part of it all, from the very start.
Wednesday of last week. When she had suddenly
awakened from her afternoon nap that day—catapulted out of a nightmare about Carol—there had
been an incredibly brilliant and violent barrage of
lightening beyond the study windows. She had staggered to the nearest window, and while she had stood
there on unsteady, arthritic legs, half-awake and half-
asleep, she'd had the eerie feeling that something

monstrous had followed her up from the world of her nightmare, something demonic with a hungry grin on its face. For a few seconds that feeling had been so strong, so real, that she had been afraid to turn around and look into the shadowy room behind her. But then she had dismissed that weird thought as nothing more than the cold residue of the nightmare. Now, of course, she knew she shouldn't have dismissed it so quickly. Something strange *had* been in the room with her—a spirit; a presence; call it what you will. It had been there. And now it was in the cat.

She left the study and hurried down the hall.

In the kitchen, she found that phone cord also chewed apart.

There was no sign of Aristophanes.

Nevertheless, Grace knew he was nearby, perhaps even close enough to be watching her. She sensed his—or *its*—presence.

She listened. The house was too silent.

She wanted to cross the few feet of open floor to the kitchen door, open it boldly, and walk away from the house. But she strongly suspected that any attempt to leave would trigger an immediate and vicious attack.

She thought about the cat's claws, teeth, fangs. It wasn't merely a house pet, not just an amusing Siamese with a cute, furry face. It was actually a tough little killing machine, too; its feral impulses lay beneath a thin veneer of domestication. It was both respected and dreaded by mice and birds and squirrels. But could it kill a grown woman?

Yes, she thought uneasily. Yes, Aristophanes could kill me if he caught me by surprise and if he went for either my throat or my eyes.

The best thing she could do was stay within the house and not antagonize the cat until she had armed herself and could feel confident of winning any battle.

The only other telephone was in the second-floor bedroom. Wary, she went upstairs, even though she knew the third extension would be out of order, too.

It was.

But there was something in the bedroom that made the journey up the stairs worthwhile. The gun. She pulled open the top drawer of her nightstand and took out the loaded pistol she kept there. She had a hunch she would need it.

A hiss. A rustle.

Behind her.

Before she could swing around and confront her adversary, he was on her. He vaulted from the floor to the bed, sprang from the bed to her back, landing with nearly enough force to knock her off balance. She tottered for a moment and almost fell forward into the bedside lamp.

Aristophanes hissed and spat and scrambled for purchase on her back.

Fortunately, she kept her feet under her. She spun around and shook herself, frantically attempting to throw him off before he could do any damage.

His claws were hooked in her clothes. Although she was wearing both a blouse and a sweater, she felt a couple of his razor-tipped nails puncturing her skin—hot little points of pain. He wouldn't let go.

She drew her shoulders up and tucked her head down, pulling her chin in tight against her chest, protecting her neck as best she could. She swung one fist up behind her back, struck only air, tried again, and hit the cat with a blow that was too weak to have done any harm.

Nevertheless, Aristophanes squealed with rage and snapped at her neck. He was foiled by her hunched shoulders and by her thick hair, which got in his mouth and gagged him.

She had never wanted anything half so much as she wanted to kill the little bastard. He was no longer the familiar pet she had loved; he was a strange and hateful beast, and she harbored no ghost of affection for him.

She wished she could use the gun she was clutching in her right hand, but there was no way she could shoot him without shooting herself, too.

She struck at him repeatedly with her left hand, her arthritic shoulder protesting sharply, painfully when she twisted her arm up and backwards at such an unnatural angle.

At least for a moment, the cat abandoned its relentless but thus far ineffective attack on her neck. It slashed its claws across her flailing fist, slicing open the skin on her knuckles.

Her fingers were instantly slick with blood. They stung so badly that her eyes started to water.

Either the sight or the odor of the blood encouraged the cat. It shrieked with savage glee.

Grace began to think the unthinkable—that she was going to lose this fight.

No!

She struggled against the grip of fear that threatened to incapacitate her, tried to clear her panic-befuddled mind, and suddenly had an idea that she thought might save her life. She stumbled toward the nearest stretch of open wall, to the left of the dresser.

The cat clung tenaciously to her back, insistently pressing its snout against the base of her skull, hissing and snarling. It was determined to force its way to her sheltered neck and rip open her jugular vein.

When Grace reached the wall, she turned her back to it, then fell against it with all her weight, slamming the cat into the plaster behind her, pinning it hard between her body and the wall, hoping to break its spine. The jolt brought a flash of pain through her shoulders and drove the animal's claws deeper into her back muscles. The cat's scream was nearly shrill enough to shatter fine crystal, and it sounded almost like the wail of a human infant. But its grip on her didn't weaken. Grace pushed away from the wall, then slammed into it a second time, and the cat wailed as before, but still held fast. She thrust herself off the wall, intending to make a third attempt to crush her adversary, but before she could fall back on him, the cat let go of her. He dropped to the floor, rolled, sprang to his feet, and scurried away from her, favoring his right foreleg.

Good. She had hurt him.

She sagged against the wall, raised the .22 pistol that was still in her right hand, and squeezed the trigger.

Nothing.

She had forgotten to switch off the safeties.

The cat hurried through the open door and disappeared into the upstairs hall.

Grace went to the door, closed it, leaned wearily against it. Gasping.

Her left hand was scratched and bleeding, and her back bore half a dozen claw punctures, but she had

won the first round. The cat was limping; he was
injured, perhaps as badly as she was, and *he* was the
one who had retreated.

No celebration, though. Not yet.

Not until she had gotten out of the house alive.
And not until she was certain that Carol was safe,
too.

●‖●‖●

After the unsettling telephone conversation he'd had
with the receptionist at Maugham & Crichton, Paul
didn't know what the hell to do.

He couldn't write. That was for sure. He couldn't
get his mind off Carol long enough to advance the
plot of his novel by so much as even one sentence.

He wanted to call Lincoln Werth, at police head-
quarters, and arrange to have a sheriff's deputy waiting at the cabin when Carol and Jane arrived up there.
He wanted them brought home. But he could imagine
the conversation he would have with Detective Werth,
and the thought of it daunted him:

"You want a deputy to meet them at the cabin?"

"That's right."

"Why?"

"I think my wife's in danger."

"What kind of danger?"

*"I think the girl, Jane Doe, might be violent.
Maybe even homicidal."*

"Why do you think that?"

*"Because under hypnosis she claimed to be Millie
Parker."*

"Who's that?"

"Millie Parker once tried to kill her mother."

"She did? When was that?"

"Back in 1905."

"Then she'd be a little old lady today, for Christ's sake. The kid's only fourteen or fifteen."

"You don't understand. Millie Parker's been dead for about seventy-six years and—"

"Wait a minute, wait a minute! What the hell are you saying? That your wife might be murdered by some kid who's been dead for most of the century?"

"No. Of course not."

"Then what do you mean?"

"I . . . don't know."

Werth would think that he had been out boozing all night, or that he had started the morning with a couple of joints of good grass.

Besides, it wasn't fair to Jane to accuse her publicly of being a potential killer. Perhaps Carol was right. Maybe the kid was just a victim. Except for what she said under hypnosis, she certainly *seemed* to be incapable of violence.

On the other hand, of all the people she could have claimed to be, why had she said that she was Millicent Parker, the would-be murderess? Where had she heard that name before. Didn't the use of it indicate latent hostility?

Paul swiveled his typing chair away from the desk and stared out the window at the gray sky. The wind was picking up by the minute. The clouds were racing westward across the sky, as if they were enormous, swift, dark ships with billowing sails the color of thunderstorms.

BLADE, BLOOD, DEATH, TOMB, KILL, CAROL.

I've got to go to the cabin, he thought with sudden decisiveness, and he got to his feet.

Maybe he was overreacting to this Millicent Parker business, but he couldn't just sit here, wondering. . . .

He went into the master bedroom to throw some things into a suitcase. After only a brief hesitation, he decided to pack his .38 revolver.

●‖●‖●

The girl said, "How much farther to the cabin?"

"Another twenty minutes," Carol said. "The whole drive usually takes just about two hours and fifteen minutes, and we're pretty much on schedule."

The mountains were cool and green. Some trees had already been touched by the artful hand of autumn, and most—all but the evergreens—would change the color of their leaves during the next few weeks. Today, however, the predominant shade was still green, with a smattering of gold here and there, an occasional touch of red. The edge of the forest— wherever the meadow or the roadway met the trees— was decorated with a few end-of-the-season wildflowers, blue and white and purple.

"It's beautiful up here," Jane said as they followed the two-lane county road around a curve. The right-hand bank, which sloped down to the macadam, was covered with vividly green clusters of rhododendron shrubs.

"I love the Pennsylvania mountains," Carol said. She felt more relaxed now than she had in weeks. "It's so peaceful here. Wait till you've been at the cabin a day or two. You'll forget the rest of the world exists."

They came out of the curve onto an ascending straightaway, where the interlocking branches of the trees formed a tunnel over portions of the lane. At

those points where the trees parted sufficiently to provide a glimpse of the sky, there was nothing to be
seen but massive, gray-black clouds clotted together
in surging, ugly, threatening formations.

"I sure hope it doesn't rain and spoil our first day
here," Jane said.

"Rain won't spoil anything," Carol assured her.
"If we're forced to stay inside, we'll just throw a
whole bunch of logs in the big stone fireplace and
roast some hot dogs *in*doors. And we have a closetful
of games to help us pass rainy days. Monopoly, Scrabble, Clue, Risk, Battleship, and at least a dozen others. I think we'll be able to avoid cabin fever."

"It's going to be *fun*," Jane said enthusiastically.

The canopy of trees parted overhead, and the September sky churned darkly.

11

GRACE sat on the edge of the bed, holding the .22 pistol, considering her options. She didn't have many.

In fact, the more she thought about it, the more it seemed to her that the cat had a better chance of winning this duel than she did.

If she attempted to leave the house by way of the bedroom window, she would surely break a leg and probably her neck as well. If she had been only twenty years younger, she might have tried it. But at seventy, with her swollen joints and brittle bones, jumping from a second-floor window onto a concrete patio could only end in misery. Anyway, the point wasn't just to get out of the house, but to get out in one piece, so she could make it across town to Carol's and Paul's place.

She could open the window and start screaming

for help. But she was afraid that Aristophanes—or the thing using Aristophanes's body—would attack anyone who showed up and tried to assist her, and she didn't want a neighbor's death on her conscience.

This was her battle. No one else's. She would have to fight it alone.

She considered all the routes by which she might possibly leave the house once she had reached the bottom floor—if she reached the bottom floor—but no particular route seemed less dangerous than any other. The cat could be anywhere. Everywhere. The bedroom was the only safe place in the house. If she ventured out of this sanctuary, the cat would be waiting for her and would attack her, regardless of whether she tried to exit the house by the front door, the kitchen door, or one of the ground-floor windows. It would be crouched in one shadow or another, perhaps perched atop a bookcase or cupboard or hutch, tensed and ready to launch itself down onto her startled, upturned face.

She had the gun, of course. But the cat, stealthy by nature, would always have the advantage of surprise. If it got just a two- or three-second lead on her, if she was only that little bit slower to react than was the cat, it would have ample time to fasten onto her face, tear open her throat, or gouge her eyes out with its quick, stiletto claws.

Strangely, though she had accepted the doctrine of reincarnation, though she now knew beyond doubt that there was some kind of life after death, she nevertheless feared dying. The certainty of eternal life in no way diminished the value of *this* life. Indeed, now that she could discern godlike machinery just below the visible surface of the world, her life seemed to have more meaning and purpose than ever before.

She didn't want to die.

However, although the odds of her leaving the house alive were, at best, only fifty-fifty, she couldn't stay in the bedroom indefinitely. She had no water, no food. Besides, if she didn't get out of here in the next few minutes, she might be too late to be of any help to Carol.

If Carol is killed simply because I lack the courage to face that damned cat, she thought, *then I might as well be dead anyway.*

She switched off the two safeties on the pistol.

She got up and went to the door.

For nearly a minute she stood with one ear pressed to the door, listening for scratching noises or other indications that Aristophanes was nearby. She heard nothing.

Holding the pistol in her right hand, she used her bloody, claw-torn left hand to turn the knob. She opened the door with the utmost caution, half an inch at a time, expecting the cat to dart through the opening the instant it was wide enough to admit him. But he didn't.

Finally, reluctantly, she poked her head out into the hall. Looked left. Right.

The cat wasn't anywhere in sight.

She stepped into the hall and paused, afraid to move away from the bedroom door.

Go! she told herself angrily. Move your ass, Gracie!

She took a step toward the head of the stairs. Then another step. Trying to be quiet.

The stairs appeared to be a mile away.

She looked behind her.

Still no Aristophanes.

Another step.

This was going to be the longest walk she had ever taken.

●ll●ll●

Paul latched his suitcase, picked it up, turned away from the bed—and jumped, startled, when the entire house shook as if a wrecker's ball had struck the side of it.

THUNK!

He looked up at the ceiling.

THUNK! THUNK! THUNK!

During the past five days there had been no hammering to disturb the peace. He hadn't entirely forgotten about it, of course; he still occasionally wondered where that mysterious sound had come from. For the most part, however, he had put it out of his mind; there had been other things to worry about. But now—

THUNK! THUNK! THUNK!

The nerve-fraying noise reverberated in the windows and bounced off the walls. It seemed to vibrate in Paul's teeth and bones, too.

THUNK!

After spending days trying to identify the source of that sound, understanding came to him unexpectedly, in a flash. *It was an ax.* It was not a hammering, which was how he had been thinking of it. No. There was a sharp edge to it, a brittle, cracking quality at the end of each blow. It was a *chopping* sound.

THUNK!

Being able to identify the noise did absolutely nothing to help him understand where it was coming from. So it was an ax instead of a hammer. So what? He still couldn't make sense of it. Why were the blows shaking the entire house? It would have to be the mythical Paul Bunyan's ax to have such a tremendous impact. And regardless of whether it was a hammer or an ax or even, for Christ's sake, a *salami*, how could the sound of it issue from thin air?

Suddenly, inexplicably, he thought of the meat cleaver that Louise Parker had buried in the throat of her maniacal daughter back in 1905. He thought about the freakish lightning strikes at Alfred O'Brian's office; the strange intruder he had seen on the rear lawn during the thunderstorm that evening; the Scrabble game two nights ago (BLADE, BLOOD, DEATH, TOMB, KILL, CAROL); Grace's two prophetic dreams. And he knew beyond doubt—without understanding *how* he knew—that the sound of the ax was the thread that sewed together all these recent extraordinary events. Intuitively, he knew that an ax would be the instrument by which Carol's life would be endangered. He didn't know how. He didn't know why. But he *knew*.

THUNK! THUNK!

A painting popped off its wall hook and clattered to the floor.

The river of blood in Paul's veins turned winter-cold.

He had to get to the cabin. Fast.

He started toward the bedroom door, and it slammed shut in front of him. No one had touched it. There had been no sudden draft that might have moved it. One moment the door was standing wide open, and the next instant it was flung shut as if it had been shoved hard by an invisible hand.

Out of the corner of his eye, Paul saw something move. Heart banging, breath trapped in his constricted throat, he twisted around toward the movement and instinctively raised his suitcase to partially shield himself.

One of the two heavy, mirrored closet doors was sliding open. He expected someone to step out of the closet, but when the door was all the way open, he could see nothing in there except clothes on hangers. Then it slid shut, and the other door slid open. Then both of them started sliding at the same time, one crossing behind the other, back and forth, back and forth on their silent plastic wheels.

THUNK! THUNK!

A lamp crashed over on one of the nightstands.

Another painting fell off the wall.

THUNK!

On the dresser, two porcelain figurines—a ballerina and her male dancing partner—began to circle one another, almost as if they had come to life and were performing for Paul. They moved slowly at first, then faster, faster, until they were swept into the air and tossed halfway across the room and dashed to the floor.

●‖●‖●

The cabin was constructed of logs and was nestled in the cool shadows beneath the trees. It had a long, covered, screened porch out front and an excellent view of the lake.

It was one of ninety vacation cabins tucked into the scenic mountain valley, each on an acre or half-acre of its own. They were all built along the south shore of the lake and were reachable only by way of a private, gated, gravel-surfaced road that curved around the water. Some of the cabins were made of logs, like the one Paul and Carol had bought, but there were also white clapboard New England models, modern A-frames, and a few that resembled small Swiss chalets.

At the end of her own graveled drive, which branched off the community road, Carol parked the car near the front door of the cabin. She and Jane got out and stood for a moment in companionable silence, listening to the stillness, breathing the wonderfully fresh air.

"It's lovely," Jane said at last.

"Isn't it, though?"

"So quiet."

"It isn't always. Not when most of the cabins are in use. But right now there's probably no one here except Peg and Vince Gervis."

"Who're they?" Jane asked.

"The caretakers. The homeowner's association pays their salaries. They live year-round in the last cabin, out at the end of the lake. In the off season, they run a couple of inspection tours every day, just keeping a lookout for fire and vandals and whatnot. Nice people."

Above the distant north shore of the lake, lightning blazed across the malevolent sky. A clap of thunder fell from the clouds and rolled across the water.

"We better get the suitcases and the food out of the car before we have to unload everything in the rain," Carol said.

●‖●‖●

Grace expected to be attacked on the stairs, for that was where she would find it most difficult to defend herself. If the cat frightened her and caused her to lose her balance, she might fall. If she fell, she would probably break a leg or a hip, and while she was temporarily stunned by the shock and pain of the fall, the cat would be all over her, tearing, biting. Therefore, she descended the stairs sideways, with her back against the wall, so she could look both ahead and behind.

But Aristophanes did not show up. Grace reached the downstairs hall without incident.

She looked both ways along the hall.

To reach the front door, she had to pass the open door of the study and the archway that led to the living room. The cat could bolt out of either place as she was passing by and could leap for her face before she would have time to spot him, aim the pistol, and pull the trigger.

To reach the other door, the one at the back of the house, she had to go right, along the hallway, past the open dining room door, into the kitchen. That route didn't look any less dangerous.

The rock and the hard place, she thought unhappily. The devil and the deep blue sea.

Then she remembered that her car keys were in the kitchen, hanging on the pegboard beside the back door, and that settled it. She would have to leave through the kitchen.

She moved cautiously along the hall until she came to a wall mirror, beneath which stood a narrow, decorative table. There were two tall vases on the table, bracketing the mirror. She picked up one of them in her injured left hand and sidled toward the open dining room door.

She paused before reaching the doorway, listened. Silence.

She leaned forward and risked her eyes by peering into the dining room. She could not see any sign of the cat. That didn't mean it wasn't in there. The drapes were half drawn, and the day was gloomy; there were lots of shadows, many places where a cat could hide.

For the purpose of creating a diversion in the event that Aristophanes *was* in one of those shadows, Grace pitched the vase inside. As it landed with a loud crash, she stepped across the threshold just far enough to grasp the doorknob, then pulled the door shut as she backed quickly into the hallway again. Now, if the cat was in there, it would bloody well have to *stay* in there.

She heard no noise from the dining room, which probably meant she hadn't managed to trap the elusive beast. If he'd been in there, he would have been squealing with rage and scratching at the inside of the closed door by now. Most likely, she had only wasted time and energy with her little trick. But at least there was now one downstairs room to which she could turn her back with impunity.

Repeatedly glancing left and right, forward and back, she crept to the kitchen door, hesitated, then stepped through it, the gun thrust out in front of her. She looked the room over slowly, thoroughly, before venturing farther. The small table and chairs. The humming refrigerator. The dangling, cat-chewed phone cord. The gleaming chrome fixtures on the oven. The double sinks. The white countertops. The small countertop wine rack. The cookie jar and the breadbox lined up beside the wine.

Nothing moved.

The refrigerator motor shut off, and the subsequent

quiet was deep, unbroken.

Okay, she thought. Grit your teeth and move, Gracie.

She walked silently across the room, her eyes sweeping every niche, every nook: the opening under the built-in writing desk, the narrow space beside the refrigerator, the blind spot beyond the end of one row of cabinets. No cat.

Maybe I hurt him worse than I thought I did, she told herself hopefully. Maybe I didn't just lame the bastard. Maybe he crawled away and died.

She reached the back door.

She didn't dare breathe for fear her own breathing would mask whatever furtive sounds the cat might make.

A ring of keys, including those for the car, hung on a small oval pegboard beside the door. She slipped it off the hook.

She reached for the doorknob.

The cat hissed.

Grace cried out involuntarily and swung her head to the right, in the direction of the sound.

She was standing at one end of the long row of cabinets. At the far end, the wine rack and the breadbox and the cookie jar were lined up side by side; she had seen them from a front-on angle when she had first come into the room. Now she had a side view. From this angle she saw something she couldn't have seen from in front: The cookie jar and breadbox, which usually rested snug against the wall behind the counter, had been moved out a few inches. The cat had squeezed in behind those two objects, muscling them slowly out of its way. It had crouched in that hiding place, its butt against the wine rack, facing out toward the kitchen door. It was approximately twelve

feet from her, and then it wasn't even that far away
because it launched itself across the counter, hissing.

The confrontation was over in a few seconds, but
during those seconds, time seemed to slow to a crawl,
and Grace felt as if she were trapped in a slow-motion
film. She stumbled backwards, away from the counter
and the cat, but she didn't get far before she collided
with a wall; as she moved, she raised the gun and
fired two rounds in quick succession. The cookie jar
exploded, and wood chips flew off one of the cabinet
doors. But the cat kept coming, coming, in slow-
motion strides across the slippery tile countertop, its
mouth gaping and its fangs bared. She realized that
hitting such a small, quick target was not easy, even
at such short range as this. She fired again, but she
knew the gun was wavering in her hand, and she
wasn't surprised when she heard the bullet ricochet—
making a high, piercing *eeeee*—off something wide
of the mark. To her terror-heightened perceptions, the
echoes of the ricochet continued to infinity: *eeeee,
eeeee, eeeee, eeeee, eeeee*.... Then the cat reached
the end of the counter and leapt into the air, and Grace
fired again. This time she hit the mark. The cat yelped.
The bullet had sufficient impact to deflect the animal
only an instant before it would have landed, scratching
and biting, on her face. It was pitched back and to
the left as if it were a bundle of rags. It slammed into
the kitchen door and dropped stonelike to the floor,
where it lay silent and motionless

●ıı●ıı●

Paul couldn't decide what the poltergeist intended to
accomplish by its impressive displays of power. He
didn't know whether or not he had anything to fear

from it. Was it trying to delay him, trying to keep him here until it was too late for him to help Carol? Or perhaps it was urging him on, trying its best to convince him that he must go to the cabin immediately.

Still holding the suitcase in one hand, he approached the bedroom door that had been flung shut by the unseen presence. As he reached for the knob, the door began to rattle in its frame—gently at first, then fiercely.

Thunk ... thunk ... thunk ... THUNK!

He jerked his hand back, unsure what he ought to do.

THUNK!

The sound of the ax was coming from the door now, not from overhead, as it had been. Although the solid-core, raised-panel, fir door was a formidable barrier rather than just a flimsy Masonite model, it shook violently and then cracked down the middle as if it were constructed of balsa wood.

Paul backed away from it.

Another crack appeared, parallel to the first, and chips of wood flew into the room.

Sliding closet doors and flying porcelain figurines might be the work of a poltergeist, but this was something else again. Surely no spirit could chop apart a heavy door like this. There *had* to be someone swinging a very real ax against the other side.

Paul felt defenseless. He scanned the room for makeshift weapons, but he saw nothing useful.

The .38 revolver was in the suitcase. He wouldn't be able to get to it in time to defend himself with it, and he wished fervently that he had kept the gun in his hand.

THUNKTHUNKTHUNKTHUNK!

The bedroom door exploded inward in half a dozen large pieces and countless smaller chunks and scraps.

He threw one arm over his face to protect his eyes. Wood rained down on all sides of him.

When he lowered his arm, he saw there was no one standing beyond the doorway, no man with an ax. The chopper-of-doors was, after all, the unseen presence.

THUNK!

Paul stepped over a shattered section of the door and went out into the hallway

● || ● || ●

The fuse box was in the kitchen pantry. Carol engaged all the breaker switches, and the lights came on.

There was no telephone. That was virtually the only modern convenience the cabin lacked.

"Do you think it's chilly in here?" Carol asked.

"A little."

"We have a bottled-gas furnace, but unless it's *really* cold, the fireplace is nicer. Let's bring in some firewood."

"You mean we've got to cut down a tree?"

Carol laughed. "That won't be necessary. Come see."

She led the girl outside, to the rear of the cabin, where an open porch ended in steps leading down to a short rear yard. The yard met the edge of a small meadow where the grass was knee-deep, and the meadow climbed up toward a wall of trees fifty yards away.

When Carol saw that familiar landscape, she stopped, surprised, remembering the dream that had spoiled her sleep several nights last week. In the nightmare, she had been running through one house, then through another house, then across a mountain meadow, while something silvery flickered in the darkness behind her. At the time, she had not realized that the meadow in the dream was *this* meadow.

"Something wrong?" Jane asked.

"Huh? Oh. No. Let's get that firewood."

She led the girl down the porch steps and to the left, to where a woodshed was attached to the southwest corner of the cabin.

Thunder rumbled in the distance. The rain hadn't begun to fall yet.

Carol keyed open the heavy-duty padlock on the woodshed, took it off the hasp, and slipped it in her jacket pocket. There would be no need to replace it until they were ready to return to Harrisburg, nine or ten days from now.

The woodshed door creaked open on unoiled hinges. Inside, Carol tugged on the chain-pull light, and a bare hundred-watt bulb revealed stacks of dry cordwood being protected from inclement weather.

A scuttle for carrying firewood hung from a ceiling hook. Carol got it down and handed it to the girl. "If you fill it up four or five times, we'll have more than enough wood to last us until tomorrow morning."

By the time Jane returned from taking the first scuttle-load into the cabin, Carol was at the chopping block, using an ax to split a short log into four sticks.

"What're you doing?" the girl asked, stopping well

out of the way and staring warily at the ax.

"When I build a fire," Carol said, "I put kindling on the bottom, a layer of these splits on top of that, and then the full logs to crown it off. It never fails to burn well that way. See? I'm a regular Daniel Boone."

The girl scowled. "That ax looks awful sharp."

"Has to be."

"Are you sure it's safe?"

"I've done it lots of times before, here and at home," Carol said. "I'm an expert. Don't worry, honey. I'm not going to accidently amputate my toes."

She picked up another short log and started to split it into quarters.

Jane went to the woodshed, giving the chopping block a wide berth. When she returned, carrying her second scuttle-load to the house, she repeatedly glanced over her shoulder, frowning.

Carol began quartering another log.

THUNK!

●II●II●

Carrying his suitcase, Paul walked down the second-floor hall to the stairway, and the poltergeist went with him. On both sides, doors opened and slammed shut, opened and slammed shut, again and again, all by themselves and with such tremendous force that it sounded as if he were walking through a murderous barrage of cannon fire.

As he descended the stairs, the chandelier at the top of the well began describing wide circles on the end of its chain, stirred by a breeze that Paul could not feel or moved by a hand that had no substance.

On the first floor, paintings were flung off walls as he passed by. Chairs toppled over. The living room sofa rocked wildly on its four graceful wooden legs. In the kitchen, the overhead utensil rack shook; pots and pans and ladles banged against one another.

By the time he reached the Pontiac in the garage, he knew he didn't have to bother taking the entire suitcase to the mountains. He hadn't wanted to go charging into the cabin with just a gun and the clothes on his back, for if nothing had been wrong, he would have looked like an idiot, and he would have done Jane a grave injustice. But now, because of the call from Polly at Maugham & Crichton, and because of the astounding display put on by the poltergeist, he knew that *everything* was wrong; there was no chance whatsoever that he would reach the cabin only to discover that all was peaceful. He would be walking into a nightmare of one kind or another. No doubt about it. So he opened the suitcase on the garage floor beside the car, took out the loaded revolver, and left the rest of his stuff behind.

As he was backing out of the driveway, he saw Grace Mitowski's blue Ford turn the corner, too fast. It angled toward the curb in front of the house, scraping its sidewalls so badly that blue-white smoke rose from them.

Grace was out of the car the instant it stopped. She rushed to the Pontiac, moving faster than Paul had seen her move in years. She pulled open the front, passenger-side door and leaned in. Her hair was in complete disarray. Her face was eggshell white and spattered with blood.

"Good God, Grace, what's happened to you?"

"Where's Carol?"

"She went to the cabin."

"Already?"

"This morning."

"Damn? Exactly when?"

"Three hours ago."

Grace's eyes contained a haunted expression. "The girl went with her?"

"Yes."

She closed her eyes, and Paul could see she was on the edge of panic, trying to deal with it and calm herself. She opened her eyes and said, "We've got to go after them."

"That's where I'm headed."

He saw her eyes widen as she noticed the revolver lying on the car seat beside him, the muzzle pointed forward, toward the dashboard.

She raised her eyes from the gun to his face. "You know what's happening?" she asked, surprised.

"Not really," he said, putting the gun in the glove compartment. "All I know for sure is that Carol's in trouble. Damned serious trouble."

"It's not just Carol we've got to worry about," Grace said. "It's both of them."

"Both? The girl, you mean? But I think the girl's the one who's going to—"

"Yes," Grace said. "She's going to try to kill Carol. But she might be the one who ends up dead. Like before."

She got in the car and pulled the door shut.

"Like before?" Paul said. "I don't—" He saw her blood-crusted hand. "That needs medical attention."

"There's no time."

"What the hell's happening?" he demanded, his fear for Carol briefly giving way to frustration. "I know something strange is going on, but I don't know what in Christ's name it is."

"I do," she said. "I know. In fact I know a lot more than maybe I want to know."

"If you've got anything that makes sense, anything concrete," he said, "we should call the cops. They can put in a call to the sheriff's department up there and get help sent out to the cabin real fast, faster than we can get there."

"What I've got, my information, is harder than concrete, so far as I'm concerned," Grace said. "But the police wouldn't see it the same way I do. They'd say I was just a senile old fool. They'd want to lock me up in a nice safe place for my own good. At best, they'd laugh at me."

He thought about the poltergeist—the sound of the ax, the splintering door, the airborne ceramic figurines, the toppling chairs—and he said, "Yeah. I know exactly what you mean."

"We'll have to handle this ourselves," Grace said. "Let's get rolling. I can tell you everything I know on the way. Each minute we waste, I just get sicker and sicker, thinking about what might be happening in the mountains."

Paul backed the car into the street and drove away from the house, heading for the nearest freeway entrance. When he was on the open highway, he floored the accelerator, and the car rocketed ahead.

"How long does it usually take to get there?" Grace asked.

"About two hours and fifteen minutes."
"Too long."
"We'll do better than that."
The speedometer needle touched eighty.

12

THEY had brought a lot of food in cardboard cartons and ice chests. They transferred all of those items to the cupboards and refrigerator, agreeing to forgo lunch altogether in order to indulge themselves guiltlessly in a glutton's dinner.

"All right," Carol said, producing a list from one of the kitchen drawers, "here's what we need to do to make this place livable." She read from the list: "Remove plastic dropcloths from furniture; dust everything; scrub the kitchen sink; clean the bathroom; and put sheets and blankets on the beds."

"You call this a *vacation*?" Jane asked.

"What's wrong? Doesn't that sound like a fun agenda to you?"

"Thrilling."

"Well, the cabin's not enormous. The two of us will go through the list of chores in an hour or an hour and a half."

They had barely started when they were interrupted by a knock at the door. It was Vince Gervis, the colony's caretaker. He was a big, barrel-chested man with enormous shoulders, enormous biceps, enormous hands, and a smile to match the rest of him.

"Just makin' my rounds," he said. "Saw your car. Thought I'd say hello." Carol introduced him to Jane and said she was a niece (a convenient white lie), and there was some polite chitchat, and then Gervis said, "Dr. Tracy, where's the *other* Dr. Tracy? I'd like to give him my best, too."

"Oh, he isn't with us right now," Carol said. "He's coming up on Sunday, after he finishes some important work he couldn't just put aside."

Gervis frowned.

Carol said, "Is something wrong?"

"Well . . . me and the missus was plannin' to go into town to do some shoppin', maybe see a movie, eat a restaurant meal. It's what we generally do on Friday afternoons, you see. But there isn't another soul up here besides you and Jane. Will be tomorrow, bein' as it's a Saturday, and seein' as if the weather don't get too bad so that everybody stays to home. But there's no one else so far today except you."

"Don't worry about us," Carol said. "We'll be fine. You and Peg go on into town like you planned."

"Well . . . I'm not sure I like the idea of you two ladies out here all by your lonesome, twenty miles from other folks. Nosir, I don't like it much."

"Nobody's going to bother us, Vince. The road's gated; you can't even get in without a key card."

"Anybody can *walk* in if he's willin' to go overland just a little ways."

Carol required several minutes and a lot of words to reassure him, but at last he decided that he and his wife would keep to their usual Friday schedule.

Shortly after Vince left, the rains came. The soft roar of a hundred million droplets striking a hundred million rustling leaves was soothing to Carol.

But Jane found the noise somewhat unpleasant. "I don't know why," she said, "but the sound makes me think of fire. Hissing . . . just like a lot of flames eating up everything in sight. Sizzle, sizzle, sizzle . . ."

●II●II●

The rain forced Paul to slow down to sixty, which was still too fast for highway conditions, but the situation called for the taking of some risks.

The windshield wipers thumped metronomically, and the tires sang softly on the wet macadam.

The day was dark and growing darker. It looked more like twilight than like midday. The wind blew obscuring curtains of rain across the treacherously wet pavement, and the gray-brown road spray flung up by other traffic hung in the air, a thick and dirty mist.

It seemed almost as if the Pontiac were a tiny vessel sailing through the deep currents of a vast, cold sea, the only pocket of warmth and light within a million miles.

Grace said, "You probably won't believe what I've got to tell you, and that would be understandable."

"After what's happened to me today," Paul said, "I'm ready to believe anything."

And maybe *that's* what the poltergeist meant to do,

he thought. Maybe it meant to prepare me for whatever story Grace has to tell. In fact, if I hadn't been delayed by the poltergeist, I would have left the house before Grace arrived.

"I'll keep it as simple and straightforward as I can," Grace said. "But it's not a simple and straightforward matter." She cradled her torn left hand in her right hand; the bleeding had stopped, and the cuts were all crusty, clotted. "It starts in 1865, in Shippensburg. The family was named Havenswood."

Paul glanced her, startled by the name.

She looked straight ahead, at the rain-sodden land through which they were rushing. "The mother was Willa Havenswood, and the daughter's name was Laura. Those two didn't get along well. Not well at all. The fault was on both sides, and the reasons for their constant bickering aren't really important here. What's important is that one day in the spring of 1865, Willa sent Laura into the cellar to do some spring cleaning, even though she knew perfectly well that the girl was deathly afraid of the cellar. It was punishment, you see. And while Laura was down there in the cellar, a fire broke out upstairs. She was trapped and burned to death. She must have died blaming her mother for putting her in that trap in the first place. Maybe she even blamed Willa for starting the fire—which she didn't. It was accidentally started by Rachael Adams, Laura's aunt. It's even possible that Laura wondered if her mother had started the fire *on purpose*, just to get rid of her. The child had emotional problems; she was capable of melodramatic notions of that sort. The mother had emotional problems, too; she was capable of *inspiring* paranoia, for sure. Anyway, Laura died a gruesome death, and we can be pretty certain that her last thought was an ardent wish for revenge. There was no way she could have known that *her mother perished in that fire, too!*"

So that's why the Havenswood identity didn't check out when Carol put the police on to it, Paul thought. They'd have had to go all the way back to the 1800s in order to find the Havenswood family. County records for that period probably don't even exist any more.

A slow-moving truck appeared out of the mists ahead, and Paul passed it. For a moment the filthy spray from the truck's big tires drummed on the side of the Pontiac, and the noise was too loud for Grace to speak above it.

When they had passed the truck, she said, "Since 1865, Laura has been pursuing revenge through at least two and probably three other lives. Reincarnation, Paul. Can you believe in that? Can you believe that in 1943, Laura Havenswood was a fifteen-year-old girl named Linda Bektermann and that the night before her sixteenth birthday she tried to kill her mother, who was Willa Havenswood reincarnated? It's a true case. Linda Bektermann went berserk and tried to ax her mother to death, but her mother turned the tables and killed the girl instead. *Laura didn't get her revenge*. And can you believe that Willa is now alive again and that she's our Carol this time? And that Laura is alive again, too?"

"Jane?"

"Yes."

●‖●‖●

Together, Carol and Jane cleaned the cabin in an hour and fifteen minutes. Carol was delighted to see that the girl was an industrious worker who took great pleasure in doing even a menial job well.

When they were finished, they poured two glasses of Pepsi to reward themselves, and they sat in the two big easy chairs that faced the mammoth fireplace.

"It's too early to start cooking dinner," Jane said. "And it's too wet out there to go for a walk, so what game do you want to play?"

"Anything that looks good to you is fine with me. You can look over all the stuff in our game closet and take your pick. But first, I think we really should get the therapy session out of the way."

"Are we going to keep that up even on vacation?" the girl asked. She was clearly uneasy about it, though she had not been noticeably uneasy before, even on the occasion of the first session, the day before yesterday.

"Of course we've got to keep on with it," Carol said. "Now that we've made a start, it's best to continue working at it, pushing and probing a little bit every day."

"Well . . . all right."

"Good. Let's turn these chairs around to face each other."

The fire flickered off to one side, creating dancing shadows on the hearth.

Outside, the rain rattled ceaselessly through the trees and pattered on the roof, and Carol realized that it *did* sound like even more fire, as Jane had said, so that they seemed to be totally surrounded by the hiss and crackle of flames.

She needed only a few seconds to put Jane into a trance this time. But as had happened during the first session, the girl needed almost two minutes to regress to a period at which memories existed for her. This time the long silence didn't disturb Carol as it had done before.

When the girl spoke at last, she used the Laura voice. "Mama? Is that you? Is that you, Mama?"

"Laura?"

The girl's eyes were squeezed shut. Her voice was tight, tense. "Is that you? Is it you, Mama? Is it?"

"Relax," Carol said.

Instead of relaxing, the girl became visibly more tense. She hunched her shoulders, fisted her hands in her lap. Lines of strain appeared in her forehead and at the corners of her mouth. She leaned away from the back of her chair, toward Carol.

"I want you to answer some questions," Carol said. "But you must be calm and relaxed first. Now, you will do exactly as I say. You will unclench your fists. You will—"

"I won't!"

The girl's eyes popped open. She leapt up out of her chair and stood before Carol, quivering.

"Sit down, honey."

"I won't do what you say! I'm sick of doing what you tell me to do, sick of your punishments."

"Sit down," Carol said softly but forcefully.

The girl glared at her. "You did it to me," she said in the Laura voice. "You put me down there in that awful place."

Carol hesitated, then decided to flow with it. "What place do you mean?"

"You *know*," the girl said accusingly. "I *hate* you."

"Where is this awful place you spoke of?" Carol persisted.

"The cellar."

"What's so awful about the cellar?"

Hatred seethed in the girl's eyes. Her lips were peeled back from her teeth in a feral snarl.

"Laura? Answer me. What's so awful about the cellar?"

The girl slapped her across the face.

The blow stunned Carol. It was sharp, painful, unexpected. For an instant she simply couldn't believe that she actually had been hit.

Then the girl hit her again. Backhanded.

And again. Harder than before.

Carol grabbed her adversary's slender wrists, but the girl wrenched loose. She kicked Carol in the shins, and when Carol cried out and sagged for an instant, the girl went for her throat. Carol fended her off, though not easily, and attempted to get up from the armchair. Jane pushed her down and fell on top of her. She felt the girl bite her shoulder, and suddenly her shock and confusion turned to fear. The chair tipped over, and they both rolled onto the floor, flailing.

●‖●‖●

The flat land through which they had been driving began to rise and form itself into gently rolling hills, but the mountains were still a long way off.

If there had been any change in the weather during the last half hour, it had been for the worse. Rain was falling harder than ever; the hard, fat pellets of water shattered like glass on the roadway, and the amorphous fragments bounced high. Paul kept the speedometer needle at eighty.

"Reincarnation," he said thoughtfully. "Just a few minutes ago, I told you that I could believe anything today, but that's wild. Reincarnation? Where in the devil did you come by this theory?"

As the windshield wipers continued to thump, and as the tires sang a shrill dirge on the rain-puddled pavement, Grace told him about the telephone calls from Leonard, the visit from the long-dead reporter, the prophetic dreams; she told him about the grim battle with Aristophanes. "I am Rachael Adams, Paul. That other life had been revealed to me so that I can stop this murderous cycle. Willa did not start the fire. *I* started it accidentally. There is no reason for the girl to seek revenge. It's all a mistake, a dark misunderstanding. If I can talk to the girl, Jane, while she's regressed to her Laura phase, I can persuade her of the truth. I know I can. I can stop all of this here, now, once and forever. Do you think I'm babbling? Senile? I don't believe I am. In fact, I *know* I'm not. And I suspect you've had some strange experiences recently that confirm what I'm telling you."

"You hit that one on the head, all right," he told her.

Nevertheless, reincarnation—being born again in a new body—it was a stunning, soul-shaking thing to accept. *There is no lasting death.* Yes, that was much harder to accept than the existence of poltergeists.

"Do you know about Millicent Parker?" he asked her.

"Never heard the name," Grace said.

The rain started falling even harder. He turned the windshield wipers up to their highest speed.

"In 1905," he told Grace, "Millie Parker attempted to kill her mother—on the night before her sixteenth birthday. Like the Linda Bektermann case, the mother ended up killing Millie, instead of the other way around. Purely self-defense. And here's what you might not realize: Under hypnosis, Jane claimed to be Laura, Millie, and then Linda Bektermann. But the names meant nothing to us."

"And again, in the Millicent Parker case," Grace said, "the girl's desire for revenge was frustrated. Yes. I knew there must be another life between Laura and Linda."

"But why this night-before-the-birthday thing that keeps cropping up?"

"Laura was looking forward to *her* sixteenth birthday with great eagerness," Grace-Rachael said. "It was going to be the best day of her life, she said. She had all sorts of plans for it—and for how her life would be changed after she attained that magical age. I think, somehow, she felt her mother's treatment of her would change once she was 'grown up.' But she died in the fire before her birthday."

"And in life after life, as her sixteenth birthday approaches, the fear of her mother and the hatred of her mother wells up from her subconscious."

Grace nodded. "From the subconscious of the girl she was in 1865, the girl—the identity—who is buried down at the bottom of Jane's psyche."

They rode in silence for a minute or two.

Paul's hands were sweaty on the steering wheel.

His mind spun as he tried to absorb the story she had told, and he had that old feeling of balancing on a tightrope high above a deep, deep, dark chasm.

Then he said, "But Carol isn't Jane's mother."

"You've forgotten something," Grace said.

"What?"

"Carol had a child out of wedlock when she was a teenager. I know she told you all about it. I'm giving away no secrets."

Paul's stomach quivered. He was cold all the way into the marrow of his bones. "My God. You mean . . . Jane is the child that Carol put up for adoption."

"I have no proof of it," Grace said. "But I bet that when the police spread their search nets wide enough, when they finally locate the girl's parents in some other state, we'll learn that she's adopted. And that Carol is her natural mother."

●ΙΙ●ΙΙ●

For what seemed like an eternity, they struggled on the floor by the hearth, grunting, twisting, the girl throwing punches, Carol trying to resist without hurting her. At last, when it became clear that Carol was unquestionably the stronger of the two and would eventually gain control of the situation, the girl shoved away from her, scrambled up, kicked her in the thigh, and ran out of the room, into the kitchen.

Carol was shocked and dazed both by the girl's unexpected violence and by the maniacal power of the blows. Her face stung, and she knew her cheeks were going to bruise. Her bitten shoulder was bleeding; a large, damp, red stain was spreading slowly down the front of her blouse.

She got up, swayed unsteadily for a moment. Then

she went after the girl. "Honey, wait!"

In the distance, outside the house, Laura's voice rose in a sharp, shrill scream: "I *haaaaaate* you!"

Carol reached the kitchen, leaned against the refrigerator. The girl was gone. The back door was open.

The sound of the rain was very loud.

She hurried to the door and looked out at the rear lawn, at the small meadow, at the forest that crowded in at the edge of the meadow. The girl had disappeared.

"Jane! Laura!"

Millicent? She wondered. Linda? What on earth *should* I call her?

She crossed the porch and went down the steps into the yard, into the pelting, cold rain. She turned right, then left, not sure where to look first.

Then Jane appeared. The girl came out of the woodshed at the southwest corner of the cabin. She was carrying an ax.

●II●II●

"*. . . and Carol is her natural mother.*"

Grace's words echoed and reechoed in Paul's head. For a moment he was incapable of speech.

He stared ahead, shocked, not really seeing the road, and he nearly ran up the back end of a sluggishly moving Buick. He jammed on his brakes. He and Grace were thrown forward, testing their seat belts. He slowed down until he could regain control of himself.

Finally, the words burst out of him like machine-

gun fire: "But how in the hell did the kid find out who
her real mother was, they don't give out that kind of
information to children her age, how did she get here
from whatever state she was living in, how did she
track us down and make it all happen like this? Good
Christ, she *did* step in front of Carol's car on purpose.
It was a setup. The whole damned thing was a setup!"

"I don't know how she found her way to Carol,"
Grace said. "Maybe her parents knew who the child's
natural mother was, and kept the name around in the
family records, in case the girl ever wanted to know
it when she grew up. Perhaps not. Perhaps anything.
Maybe she was simply drawn to Carol by the same
forces that tried to get to me through Aristophanes.
That might explain why she appeared to be in a daze
before she stepped in front of the car. But I don't
really know. Maybe we'll *never* know."

"Oh, shit," Paul said, and his voice wavered. "Oh,
no, no. Goddamn!"

"What?"

"You know how Carol is on *that* day," he said
shakily. "The day her baby was born, the baby she
gave up. She's different from the way she is every
other day of the year. Depressed, withdrawn. It's always such a bad day for her that the date's engraved
on my memory."

"On mine, too," Grace said.

"It's tomorrow," he said. "If Jane *is* Carol's child,
she'll be sixteen tomorrow."

"Yes."

"And she'll try to kill Carol today."

●II●II●

Sheets of dark rain rippled and flapped like wind-whipped canvas tents.

Carol stood on the soggy lawn, unable to move, numbed by fear, frozen by the cold rain.

Twenty feet away, the girl stood with the ax, gripping it in both hands. Her drenched hair hung straight to her shoulders, and her clothes were pasted to her. She appeared to be oblivious to the storm and the chilly air. Her eyes were owlish, as if she were high on amphetamine, and her face was distorted by rage.

"Laura?" Carol said at last. "Listen to me. You will listen to me. You will drop the ax."

"You stinking, rotten bitch," the girl said through tightly clenched teeth.

Lightning cracked open the sky, and the falling rain glittered for a moment in the stroboscopic flashes that came through from the other side of the heavens.

When the subsequent thunder rolled away and Carol could be heard, she said, "Laura, I want you to—"

"I hate you!" the girl said. She took one step toward Carol.

"Stop this right now," Carol said, refusing to retreat. "You will be calm. You will relax."

The girl took another step.

"Drop the ax," Carol insisted. "Honey, listen to me. You *will* listen to me. You are only in a trance. You are—"

"I'm going to get you this time, Mama. This time I'm not going to lose."

"I'm not your mother," Carol said. "Laura, you are—"

"I'm going to cut your goddamn head off this time, you bitch!"

The voice had changed.

It wasn't Laura's now.

It belonged to Linda Bektermann, the third identity.

"I'm going to cut your goddamn head off and put it on the kitchen table with Daddy's."

With a jolt, Carol recalled last week's nightmare. There had been a moment in the dream when she had stepped into the kitchen and had encountered two severed heads on the table, a man's and a woman's. But how could Jane know what had been in that nightmare?

Carol finally took a step backwards, then another. Although the rain was cold, she began to sweat.

"I'm only going to tell you one more time, Linda. You must put the ax down and—"

"I'm going to cut your head off and chop you into a thousand little pieces," the girl said.

And the voice now belonged to Jane.

It wasn't the voice of an identity heretofore only evident in a trance. This was *Jane's* voice. She had come out of the trance on her own power. She knew who she was. She knew who Carol was. And she *still* wanted to use the ax.

Carol edged toward the back porch steps.

The girl quickly circled in that direction, blocking access to the cabin. Then she started toward Carol, moving fast, grinning.

Carol turned and ran toward the meadow.

●ıı●ıı●

In spite of the pounding rain, which snapped with bulletlike power into the windshield, in spite of the dirty mist that hung over the road, in spite of the treacherously greasy pavement, Paul slowly pressed the accelerator all the way to the floor and swung the Pontiac into the passing lane.

"It's a mask," he said.

Grace said, "What do you mean?"

"The Jane Doe identity, the Linda Bektermann and Millie Parker identities—each of them was just a mask. A very real, very convincing mask. But a mask nonetheless. Behind the mask there was always the same face, the same person. Laura."

"And we've got to put an end to the masquerade once and for all," Grace said. "If I can just talk to her as her Aunt Rachael, I'll be able to stop this madness. I'm sure I will. She'll listen to me . . . to Rachael. That's who she was closest to. Closer than she was to her mother. I can make her understand that her mother, Willa, didn't intentionally or even accidentally start that fire back in 1865. At last she'll understand. She'll see that there's no justification for revenge. The cycle will come to an end."

"If we're in time," Paul said.

"If," Grace said.

●II●II●

Carol ran through the stinging rain and through the knee-high grass. She ran up the sloping meadow, her arms tucked in close to her side, legs pumping high, gasping for breath, each stride jarring her to the bones.

Ahead lay the forest, which seemed to be her only salvation. There were thousand of places to hide in the wilderness, countless trails on which she could

lose the girl. After all, she was somewhat familiar
with the land, but to the girl it was a strange place.

Halfway across the meadow, she risked a glance
behind her. The girl was only fifteen feet away.

Lightning slashed through the bellies of the clouds,
and the blade of the ax flashed once, twice, with a
brilliant reflection of that icy electric glow.

Carol looked straight ahead once more and redoubled her efforts to reach the trees. The meadow
was wet, spongy, and in some places slippery. She
expected to fall or at least twist an ankle, but she
reached the perimeter of the forest without trouble.
She plunged in among the trees, among the purple
and brown and black shadows, into the lush under-
growth, and she began to think there was a chance—
maybe only a very small chance, but a chance nonetheless—that she would come out of this alive.

●ΙΙ●ΙΙ●

Hunching over the steering wheel, squinting at the
rain-swept highway, Paul said, "I want one thing perfectly clear between us."

Grace said, "What's that?"

"Carol's my first concern."

"Of course."

"If we walk into the middle of a nasty situation at
the cabin, I'll do whatever's necessary to protect
Carol."

Grace glanced at the glove compartment. "You
mean . . . the gun."

"Yes. If I have to, if there's no other way, I'll use
it, Grace. I'll shoot the girl if there's no other choice."

"It's unlikely that we'll walk into the middle of a confrontation," Grace said. "Either it won't have begun yet—or it'll all be over with by the time we get there."

"I won't let her hurt Carol," he said grimly. "And if worse comes to worst, I don't want you trying to stop me."

"There are some things you should consider," Grace said.

"What?"

"First of all, it'll be just as tragic if Carol kills the girl. And that's the pattern, after all. Both Millie and Linda attacked their mothers, but *they* were the ones killed. What if that happens this time? What if Carol is forced to kill the girl in self-defense? You know she's never stopped feeling guilty about putting the baby up for adoption. She carries that on her shoulders sixteen years after the fact. So what will happen when she discovers she's killed her own daughter?"

"It'll destroy her," he said without hesitation.

"I think it very well might. And what'll it do to your relationship with Carol if *you* kill her daughter, even if you do it to save Carol's life?"

He thought about that for a moment. Then he said, "It might destroy *us*, and he shuddered.

●||●||●

For a while, no matter how tortuous the path she followed through the woods, Carol could not lose the girl. She switched from one natural trail to another, crossed a small stream, doubled back the way she had come. She moved in a crouch at all times, staying out of sight below the brush line. She made no sound that could be heard above the constant hissing of the rain. Most of the time she carefully stepped on old leaves or made her way from stone to stone, from log to log, leaving no footprints, in the damp, bare earth. Yet Jane pursued her with uncanny confidence, without hesitation, as if she were part bloodhound.

At last, however, Carol was certain she had lost the girl. She squatted under a huge pine, leaned back against the damp bark, and breathed deeply, rapidly, raggedly, while waiting for her heart to stop racing.

A minute passed. Two. Five.

The only sound was the rain drizzling down through the leaves and through the interlaced pine needles.

She became aware of the dank odor of heavy vegetation—moss and fungus and forest grass and more.

Nothing moved.

She was safe, at least for now.

But she couldn't just sit beneath the tall pine, waiting for help to arrive. Eventually, Jane would stop searching for her and would try to find a way back to the cabin. If the girl didn't get lost—which she most likely would do—if she somehow managed to return to the cabin, and if she was still in a psychotic fugue when she got there, she might murder the first person she encountered. If she took Vince Gervis by surprise, even his great size and impressive muscles would be of no use against the blade of an ax.

Carol stood up, moved away from the tree, and began to circle back toward the cabin. The keys to the Volkswagen were in her purse, and her purse was in one of the bedrooms. She had to get the keys, drive into town, and ask the county sheriff for assistance.

What went wrong? she wondered. The girl shouldn't

have become violent. There was no indication that she was capable of such a thing. The potential to kill simply was not a part of her psychological profile. Paul was right to be worried. But *why*?

Proceeding with utmost caution, expecting the girl to leap at her from behind every tree and bush, Carol needed fifteen minutes to reach the edge of the forest at a point not far from the place at which she had entered the trees with the girl in hot pursuit. The meadow was deserted. At the bottom of the slope, the cabin huddled in the pouring rain.

The kid's lost, Carol thought. All of that twisting and turning and doubling back through unfamiliar territory was too much for her. She'll never find the way home by herself.

The sheriff's men weren't going to like this one: a search in the rain, in the forest, for a violent girl who was armed with an ax. No, they weren't going to like this one at all.

Carol navigated the meadow at a run.

The rear door of the cabin was standing open, just as she had left it.

She hurried inside, slammed the door, and threw the bolt. Relief swept through her.

She swallowed a couple of times, caught her breath, and crossed the kitchen to the door that led into the living room. She was about to step across that threshold when she was stopped by a sudden, terrible certainty that she was not alone.

She jumped back, spurred by intuition more than anything else, and even as she moved, the ax swung in from the left, through the doorway. It sliced the air where she had been. If she hadn't moved, she would have been cut in half.

The girl stepped into the room, brandishing the ax. "Bitch."

Carol backed to the door that she had just latched. She fumbled behind her for the bolt. Couldn't find it.

The girl closed in.

Whimpering, Carol turned to the door, seized the latch. She sensed the ax rising into the air behind her and knew she wouldn't have time to open the door, and she jerked to one side, and the blade bit into the door just where her head would have been.

With superhuman strength, the girl wrenched the ax out of the wood.

Gasping, Carol ducked past her and ran into the living room. She looked for something with which to defend herself. The only thing available was a poker in the rack of fireplace tools. She grabbed it.

Behind her, Jane said, "I hate you!"

Carol whirled.

The girl swung the ax.

Carol brought the poker up without any time to spare, and it rang against the gleaming, viciously sharp blade, deflecting the blow.

The impact rang back the length of the poker, into Carol's hands, numbing them. She couldn't maintain her grip on the iron rod; it fell from her tingling hands.

The impact did not ring back along the wooden handle of the ax, and Jane still held that weapon with firm determination.

Carol backed up onto the wide hearth of the stone fireplace. She could feel the heat against her legs.

She had nowhere else to run.

"Now," Jane said. "Now. At last."

She lifted the ax high, and Carol cried out in an-

ticipation of the pain, and the front door was flung
open. It crashed against the wall. Paul was there. And
Grace.

The girl glanced at them but was not going to be
distracted; she brought the ax down toward Carol's
face.

Carol collapsed onto the hearth.

The ax struck the stone mantel over her head;
sparks flew.

Paul rushed at the girl, but she sensed him coming.
She turned toward him, slashed with the ax, and drove
him back.

Then turned on Carol again.

"Cornered rat," she said, grinning.

The ax came up.

This time it won't miss, Carol thought.

Someone said, "Spiders!"

The girl froze.

The ax was suspended in midair.

"Spiders!" It was Grace. "There are spiders on your
back, Laura. Oh God, they're all over your back.
Spiders! Laura, look out for the spiders!"

Carol watched, bewildered, as a look of stark terror
took possession of the girl's face.

"Spiders!" Grace shouted again. "Big, black, hairy
spiders, Laura. Get them off! Get them off your back.
Quick!"

The girl screamed and dropped the ax, which clattered against the stone hearth. She brushed frantically
at her back, twisting her arms up behind her. She was
snuffling and squealing like a very small child. "Help
me!"

"Spiders," Grace said again, as Paul picked up the
ax and put it out of the way.

The girl tried to tear off her blouse. She dropped to her knees, then fell onto her side, gibbering in terror. She writhed on the floor, brushing imaginary spiders off her body. Within a minute she seemed to be in a state of shock; she lay shuddering, weeping.

"She was always afraid of spiders," Grace said. "That was why she hated the cellar."

"The cellar?" Carol asked.

"Where she died," Grace said.

Carol didn't understand. But at the moment she didn't care. She watched the girl writhing on the floor, and she suddenly felt overwhelming pity for her. She knelt beside Jane, lifted her up, hugged her.

"You okay?" Paul asked her.

She nodded.

"Spiders," the girl said, quivering uncontrollably.

"No, honey," Carol said. "No spiders. There aren't any spiders on you. Not now. Not any more." And she looked at Grace, wondering.